Psychotherapy

The science of understanding and healing the mind

Centenary Edition

Dr N.L. Dosajh

(1916–2005)

Editors: Randeep Wadehra & Pooja Kapoor

DEDICATION

My wife Kanta
And
My sons Rajiv and Sanjiv

Dr N.L. Dosajh

CONTENTS

Introduction

This small book on psychotherapy is the result of personal experiences and conclusions of about six decades in dealing with cases of mental troubles. The cases that I handled were declared purely functional by the medical authorities, and mostly fell in the category of psychoneurosis. The method of handling mental cases illustrated in the book, is purely verbal and makes use of psychoanalytical procedures. Techniques like suggestion, sympathy, hypnosis, training of the will, sublimation, meditation, psychological testing, interview, and counselling etc., have been discussed. No medicine of any kind was administered for dealing with such cases. Whenever necessity was felt, competent medical advice was sought. In fact, most of the cases referred to the author were from highly qualified doctors.

— Dr N.L. Dosajh

Dr N.L. Dosajh

The Rise of Psychotherapy

Psychotherapy is a systematic exploration of the neurotic patient's mental processes by verbal means in order to help him regain better personal and social integration. Until the recent past, while dealing with the cases of mental illness, the emotional life of a subject was totally ignored by the doctors, as the mind was considered to be the domain of philosophers. It was only later on that the study of what is called 'life force', 'élan vital' or 'libido' became a part of clinical psychology.

When Meyer, a leading doctor, suggested that more attention ought to be paid to the mind, his suggestion was ignored by the mainstream doctors because they considered the body only to be the proper subject of their study. Mental symptoms, then, were merely thought to be the result of structural damage, degeneration of the brain, tumours of the brain and other physical disturbances.

In the seventeenth century, the blood of young sane persons used to be transfused into mentally disturbed persons with the hope that the method might cure them. Again, major surgical operations were performed and various organs from the body were removed with the hope that they would help the mental patients. These attempts were met with disastrous consequences, often ending with the life of the patient.

George Stahl, a German doctor, astounded the medical specialists, when he said, however valuable detailed anatomical knowledge might be, the body's function in life was something greater and beyond the sum of its material parts. He believed that an understanding about how the soul and the vital force worked together in the body was more important than a knowledge of physics and chemistry. He showed that disturbed emotions could interfere with the physical health of a person. It was he who gave the idea that most of the diseases are psychosomatic and that body and mind interact with each other. He, therefore, suggested that the study of both mind and body is required to deal with psychosomatic illnesses. This principle, as given by Stahl, found some acceptance in the eighteenth century. By the end of the eighteenth century, the superstitious persecution of the insane was forbidden by law, because in those days insane people were kept in prison.

Esquirol, a great psychiatrist, wrote this about French asylums, 'I have seen them naked, or covered with rags and protected only with straw from the cold damp pavement upon which they were lying, I have seen them coarsely fed, deprived of fresh air, or water to quench their thirst, and of the most necessary things of life. I have seen them delivered and abandoned to the brutal supervision of veritable jailors. I have seen them in squalid, stinking little hovels without air or light, chained in caves where wild animals would not have been confined.'

The reports given above about some of the mental hospitals show that the conditions were most appalling. They also made use of very oppressive measures. For instance, chains were used frequently to control the mentally ill. The patients were kept in very unhygienic conditions. They were generally huddled together like sheep and goats in small dingy rooms, where most of them died a lingering death. Philippe Pinel, a physician superintendent of the Bicetre Hospital in Paris, was the first to unchain his patients. He stopped the practice of bloodletting and disallowed violence.

During this time, Anton Mesmer entered the field with his idea of animal magnetism. He developed the technique which was later called mesmerism. He used this technique for the treatment of neuroses. Mesmerism became quite popular towards the end of the eighteenth century.

In the nineteenth century, hypnotism developed from mesmerism, and was used in surgery. Operations began to be performed with the aid of hypnotism. An English surgeon James Braid and Frenchmen Liebeault and Charcot studied hypnotism more thoroughly. Certain physicians in England took great interest in mesmerism and hypnotism. The main among these were Elliotson, Braid and Esdaile. The cures made through hypnotism proved more scientific than mesmerism. Meanwhile, Liebeault, who was a resident of Nancy—a town in France—had made himself familiar with the phenomena of hypnotism and animal magnetism. In the Nancy school, the methods of hypnotism involved direct suggestion of sleep. According to Bernheim, hypnosis was normal sleep and that the trance state itself was the result of suggestion. Charcot, a famous physician of Paris, put forward a theory of hypnotism that was opposed to the theory of Nancy

School. He explained hypnotism on physiological bases. He said hypnotism was a symptom of hysteria, which is a disease of the nervous system.

In 1885, Sigmund Freud came on the scene and revolutionized the science of the mind with his highly influential and controversial theories. Dr Brodie also worked with the mentally ill patients, especially hysterical, and came to the same conclusion as Freud that unconscious stimulations are primary factors in the production of symptoms of hysteria. Pierre Janet also made a number of studies of hysterical patients.

As a result of experimental findings of Freud, Janet and others, individuals like Esquirol, Tuke and Higgins changed the attitude of the public to better institutional care of the mentally ill.

Dorothea Lynde Dix, an American woman, started her campaign for the improvement of the mentally ill. John Conolly—the English medical superintendent of the Hanwell Asylum—removed all forms of mechanical restraint from the mental patients. Dr Ferrus of the Bicetre Hospital was the first to advocate occupational therapy for the mentally ill. Henry Maudsley, the great English psychiatrist, gave a philosophical history of insanity. He regarded brain merely as the organ of mind. He believed that the structural and physiological processes were indissolubly linked with both normal and abnormal mental function. He said that the whole interdependence of mind and body was for one purpose—the will of God.

In this body-mind relationship, Maudsley also took into account the influence of environment. He thus laid the foundation of the modern technique of detailed historical and clinical studies of individual mental patients. This method was later fully developed in the twentieth century by the famous American psychiatrist Adolf Meyer, Emil Kraepelin, Engen Bleuler, and Adler.

In India, too, the conditions for the treatment of mental patients were no better. The mentally ill were tortured because they were supposed to be possessed of evil spirits. They were handed over to people who practised witchcraft. It was only in the twentieth century that mental hospitals were opened in India, and psychoanalysis, analytical psychology, shock therapy, group therapy, and other scientific methods began to be employed.

New Horizons in Psychotherapy

Most of the troubles with which a psychotherapist has to deal with are of a psychosomatic nature, which can be approached in two ways: mind or body, or both. If we approach from the mental side, we have to take into consideration the whole of the psyche—its conscious as well as unconscious aspects. The conscious aspect is easy to tackle. As the trouble is at the surface level, it is apparent both to the patient as well as the clinician. But when the trouble is at the deeper level of the personal unconscious, or still deeper at the collective unconscious level, the diagnosis becomes very difficult because neither the patient nor the clinician knows the causes and the cure. Then comes the necessity of a very sensitive tool like a projective technique as Rorschach, Thematic Apperception Test, Holtzman Test, or Somatic Inkblot Series Test.

During my experience of about fifty years as a clinical psychologist, I found Somatic Inkblot Series (SIS) an excellent and very effective psycho-diagnostic tool. It is because of its special merits that it has spread all over the world in the span of a few years. It has a number of forms like: SIS-1 (20 cards set), SIS-II (62 images test) and SIS-II Video. The video test makes the procedure more interesting and dreamlike. By introducing the video technology, Cassel has widened the scope of the use of this test. This way the test can be administered to a group of persons at the same time. The video test is available on the internet.

With experience gained by using the above tests, I devised my own test called the D-Test. A detailed account is given in a section devoted especially to this test, and a number of cases are reported to illustrate the workings of my test. I have tried to combine Indian and Western methods to help patients realise an integrated personality which leads to a fuller and happier life free of psychological disorders. This is my attempt at psychosynthesis.

Psychosynthesis

One of the earliest thinkers to consider psychosynthesis in the West was Carl Jung, who proposed his ideas in his famous book, *Integration of Personality*. In India, psychosynthesis is an age-old tradition, and one of the most influential. It was propounded by Patanjali who professed the growth of an integrated personality through Yoga and meditation.

Over the centuries, others have made valuable contribution. Self-actualisation by Adler and Maslow, Functional Autonomy by Allport are some attempts in this direction. Shri Aurobindo gives a complete description of integral personality through integral yoga. Alfonso Caycedo gives his technique of Sophrotherapy where he combines the traditional methods with the modern techniques.

Assagioli elaborated on his technique of psychosynthesis in 1959, while Vaughan introduced, what he called, transpersonal therapies that are concerned with liberation and transcendence, and are more likely to aim at developing a context of self-consciousness within which the process unfolds. 'A transpersonal approach need not exclude the other types of work but hold a broader perspective. In addition to the usual therapeutic techniques, this approach also questions belief about the nature of the self and reality, and thus establishes a favourable context for healing at any level.'

Psychosynthesis is a method of integrating the various subpersonalities of the individual. The initial stage is body-mind integration. This is followed by body-mind-spirit integration. This leads to complete synthesis. How does this psychosynthesis take place, especially from body-mind to body-mind-spirit? This can be understood in terms of consciousness. Consciousness is a sort of awareness of our environments outside us and understanding various phenomena that are taking place within us. This ordinary consciousness is raised to higher levels of transcendental consciousness – cosmic, micro and unity (macro). This is effected through one of the methods of meditation or through the instructions of a Sophrotherapist. As the conscious levels rise, the various conflicts, complexes and prejudices get resolved until complete enlightenment takes place. The individual gradually attains the power of intuition, first only for occasional moments and then for all times, unless he comes to the lower level of consciousness. The various levels of consciousness have their own characteristics, which are well explained by Aurobindo, Dr Anthony Campbell, Maharishi Mahesh Yogi and Dr Harold Bloomfield.

A combination of two approaches, psychoanalytical and psychosynthetic, leads to the development of both spheres of the cerebrum of the man and makes him a 'Whole Man'. Such people may bring peace into the war-torn world and usher in a new era of peace and enlightenment.

References

i. Anthony, Campbell (1980) *States of Consciousness*, Victor Gollness Ltd., London, p. 110

ii. Assagioli, Robert (1959) *Psychosynthesis,* Psychosynthesis Research Foundation, P.O. Box 3695, Greenville, Delaware, USA.

iii. Aurobindo, Shri (1972) *The Synthesis of Yoga, Part II*, Pondicherry, Vol. 20, p. 511

iv. Bloomfield, Harold H. (1975) *TM: Discovering Inner Energy & Overcoming Stress*, Delacorte Press, New York.

v. Cassel, W.A. (1977) *Desensitization Therapy for Body Image Anxiety*, Canadian Psychiatric Association Journal, 22, 239-241.

vi. Cassel, W.A & Dubey, B.L. (1997) *Somatic Inkblot Series II/Video Manual*, SIS Centre, Anchorage, Alaska.

vii. Dosajh, N.L. (1983) *Vitalism*, Bombay Psychologist, 5:1, 136-138.

viii. Dosajh, N.L. (1983) *Psychotherapy*, Kohli Publishers, Chandigarh.

ix. Dosajh, N.L. (1998) *Somatic Inkblot Series – An Excellent Diagnostic Tool*, SIS Journal of Project Psychological & Mental Health, 5:1, 136-38.

x. Vaugham, F. (1986) *The Inward Arc*: Healing and Wholeness-psychotherapy and Spirituality, Boston, Shambhala, New Science Library.

xi. Yogi, Mahesh (1966) *The Science of Being* and *Art of Living*, International SRM Publication, London and Rishikesh.

Theories of Mental Illness

Theories of psychology and mental illness can be broadly classified into two types: Physiogenic and Psychogenic.

The Physiogenic Theory: According to this theory, in all types of mental troubles, there is a gradual impairment of the nervous system, and it may result from direct trauma like some severe injury or infection, or by indirect trauma of, say, diseases like diabetes etc.

The Psychogenic Theory: According to this theory, mental disorder is due to some intra-psychic conflict because of environmental factors. According to Freud, this intra-psychic conflict is generally of a sexual nature. To Jung, the libido is trying to adapt the individual to the environment. When there is an obstacle to be surmounted, conflict is the result. Kempt says the conflict is between unsatisfied wish of the personality, while Adler says this conflict is due to the frustration of the urge to dominate. The urge to dominate, according to Adler, springs from a feeling of inferiority because of inherent organic defect.

Psychoanalysis

Psychoanalysis mostly deals with the unconscious mind and it is to this aspect of the mind that Freud paid special attention. So, before we discuss Freud's technique, we should thoroughly understand what the unconscious mind is. According to Freud, the mind can be divided into conscious, preconscious and unconscious. He postulated that the major part of the mind, rather three-fourths of it is unconscious. The conscious mind is just the tip of the iceberg. The ideas stored in the mind are so large that all of them cannot be contained in the conscious part of the mind at a particular moment. Hence, some of the ideas keep lurking in the preconscious and can be recalled to consciousness by an effort of the memory. But then there are a number of ideas and experiences that are relegated into deeper recesses of the mind—the unconscious mind. Now, the ideas and experiences stored in this region cannot be accessed easily. It is possible to delve into the deep unconscious by special techniques like free association and hypnoanalysis.

As the unconscious has proved to be very controversial, Freud had faced severe criticism when he proposed his theory. Undeterred, Freud tried to prove the existence of the unconscious thus:

1. The ideas in the unconscious are frequently charged with emotions. Freud demonstrated that by special methods these ideas together with accompanying emotions can be revived.

2. Many of those conscious and unconscious motives of life are incompatible. Under anaesthesia and in a state of somnambulism this fact becomes apparent.

3. Under hypnotic suggestion, a subject is trained to perform certain acts which he cannot perform consciously. On coming out of hypnosis, he can perform those actions quite easily although he has no recollection of learning them (as they were 'taught'

under hypnosis). To Freud, this was a proof of the unconscious mind.

4. Lost memories sometimes return to consciousness through a process of spontaneous association, although when one tries actively to recollect them, he fails.

5. The committing of errors in writing and showing slips of tongue, Freud attributed to buried feelings and ideas in the unconscious. At first, Freud thought that the unconscious was purely autogenic, i.e., its contents are derived entirely from the individual's experiences. Later on, he added that antenatal and social experiences were also stored within the unconscious mind. He attributed this to phylogenesis, i.e., due to racial evolution. Freud did this only after Jung gave the idea of racial unconscious. According to Freud, unconscious feelings begin to emerge only after the repressive forces are broken down. And this process of breaking down of the repressive forces and getting at the unconscious is what Freud called psychoanalysis.

Some of the chief characteristics of the unconscious according to Freud are:

1. It is entirely amoral and egocentric.
2. It is not delimited by time or space.
3. It is not influenced by negation.
4. It is dominated by the pleasure-pain principle.
5. Its energy is transferable from one idea to another.

6. An unconscious idea cannot reach the preconscious or conscious part of the mind until and unless there is a verbal representation attached to it.
7. It is illogical.
8. It is infantile and largely sexual.

Freud divided the mind into Ego, Superego and Id. According to Freud, the Id is unconscious, amoral, dominated by the pleasure-pain principle and illogical; it contains all repressed ideas, embodies all phylogenetic deposits, i.e., enregistration of racial evolution, is the great storehouse of the libido or love energy, life and death instincts and it promotes primitive habit formation.

The Ego is largely conscious, logical, and deals with reality. It acts as an intermediary between external reality, instinctive pressure from the Id and control from the Superego. Ego adopts moral standards, recognizes time relations, is verbalized and goes to sleep, but is responsible for the censoring of the dreams.

The Superego scrutinizes and controls the Ego. Superego is mainly formed due to the parent of the same sex. Superego acts like a critic all the time. Whenever the Ego shows weakness, the Superego produces a sense of guilt in the subject. The Ego may then try to repress that guilt-sense. In fact, the Ego has the thankless task of striking a balance between the demands of the Id and the censorship of the Superego.

The Libido

According to Freud, the libido is the energy of those instincts which have to do with all that may be comprised under the word love. Libido is much wider than sexual urge. Freud, however, maintains that sexual love cannot be separated from, on the one hand, self-love and, on the other, love for parents and children, friendship and love for humanity in general, also devotion to concrete objects and abstract ideas. Our justification, he continues, lies in the fact that psychoanalytic research has taught us that all these tendencies are an expression of the same instinctive activities. Jung's definition of libido is slightly different. He uses this term in a much wider sense. For him, libido means the total strivings of the individual. So, Jung's libido is equivalent to Bergson's élan vital or McDougall's horme. According to Freud, libido is present in all human beings, but the intensity of the libidinal energy varies from individual to individual and, in the same individual, at different times and during different physiological and psychological conditions. Thus, libidinal energy can be stimulated through various zones called erotogenic. These zones are the ones meant for nutrition, excretion and procreation. Freud believes that the child is born with the capacity for sexual excitability. In the early stages, it is egocentric and asocial. But soon the child begins to overcome these tendencies. The tendency of egocentrism is very prominent between the ages of three and five. In the early stages of a child's life, his behaviour is mostly dictated by libidinal gratification. He is full of self-love and self-importance. He directs his aggressions and destructive tendencies against all those whom he loves. When the child fails to face a situation, he withdraws and enters his inner world of fantasy. Because of his erotic and aggressive impulses, he begins to have unconscious guilt. If the child fails to manage his aggressive impulses, the ego tries to repress the ideas to which these impulses are attached, but the Id maintains the impulses. This results in a conflict, and neurosis develops.

According to Freud, the psychosexual development of the child takes place in the following manner. At birth, there is a diffused distribution of libido. Then the first erotogenic zone is established, namely the lips. After that, erotization passes to excretory passages and later to the genital area by the age the child reaches the phallic primacy stage. This stage is followed by a period of primacy 'latency' in which no new erotic zones are established. At puberty, the genital primacy stage is reached. During the period of adolescence, the said order of the development of the erogenous zones is repeated; there is a very close resemblance in these two periods. If a certain phase is very well marked in infancy, it will be equally well marked during adolescence. It is not known why these phases are repeated. This much is clear that the development of oral and genital zones in infancy makes the process pleasurable for the child. This helps in the growth of his self since the child takes interest in his nutrition. During adolescence, the genital zone develops and that very energy now helps in the preservation of the race. So, the main purpose of the libidinal energy is preservation, first of the self and then of the race.

People have been classified on the basis of the said three types of infantile and adolescent eroticism. The normal character has been defined as an organized series of behaviour reactions, which secure equilibrium between Id tendencies and surrender to reality. These reactions begin in the period of infantile sexuality and form a continuous series of adaptations. According to another writer, the oral and anal types of character cannot do so. There are two types of character, viz., (a) those who have experienced pleasure in sucking to their maximum; and (b) those whose urge for sucking was thwarted. The first group becomes optimistic, carefree and finds pleasure in taking. The second is impatient, demanding, dependent and pessimistic. The anal character is also classified into two types. The first feels pleasure in the act of defecation and the second feels pleasure from the faecal material itself. According to Freud, the following are the main features of the anal character. He shows orderliness in bodily cleanliness, reliability, conscientiousness in performance of petty duties fastidiously. He is avaricious, obstinate and may become defiant, irritable and vindictive. The anal character is generally sadistic. That is why we speak of such characteristics as anal sadistic. Such a subject may think that he is superior to others and no one else can do things as good as he does. He is generally individualistic and becomes a good organizer.

The oral personality, on the other hand, is hasty, quick, restless and impatient. The oral character accepts new ideas readily, whereas the anal character is conservative and reserved. The following table of the character qualities of anal character is reproduced from Professor Flugel's *Introduction to Psychoanalysis*.

Displacements and Sublimations

Retention

Postponement

Defiance

Obstinacy

Miserliness

Love of Possessions

Desire to Collect

Dislike of Waste

Production

Concentration (especially after postponement)

Generosity

Extravagance

Contamination

Untidiness

Noise (music)

Leaving Mark

Sadistic

Destruction

Speech

Writing

Painting

Manipulation

Moulding

Cooking

Chemistry

Photography

Building

Engineering

Product

Child

Money

Papers

Reaction Formation

Tidiness

Organization

Pedantry

Clear Thinking

Thoroughness

Punctuality

Cleanliness

Washing

Cleaning

Preventing Accumulation

Fear of Contamination (e.g. of self or nature)

Purity

Reality

Control

Strong Will (resisting temptation)

Ascetism

The 'genital character' shows maturity and is at a higher stage of psychosexual development. It is said that the oral stage brings with it an optimism and energy, the anal stage inculcates the power of endurance and the genital stage provides the drive for effectiveness. The three stages are localized as oral, anal and genital. Corresponding to these zones, there are three stages in the direction of the libido: the first is autoerotic; the second, narcissism and the third stage is allo-erotic. In the first stage, the child is both the lover and the loved, and the behaviour is controlled purely by the Id impulses. This is, as we call it, a purely narcissistic stage. Then a portion of the libido gets detached and is attached to the outside objects. Narcissism may express itself in autoerotic practices but it is not necessary. According to Freud, narcissism is the libidinous component of egoism. From narcissism, the individual gradually seeks an external object of love, starting from his family members to relatives and friends. The individual begins to have conscious and unconscious sexual fantasies about them. This results in complications like Oedipus Complex in which there is a sexual desire on the part of the child towards the parent of the opposite sex together with rivalry towards the one of its own.

According to Freud, the future development of the child depends upon the fact as to how he resolves the complex. His future character and development are very much dependent upon the way this complex is resolved. The future neurosis, if any, is also traced to this complex by

Freudian psychoanalysis. According to Freud, 'Distinct traces are probably to be found in most people of an early partiality on the part of a daughter for her father or on the part of a son for his mother. But it must be assumed to be more intense from the very first in the case of those children whose constitution marks them down for a neurosis, who develop prematurely and have a craving for love.' Again, Freud writes, 'We recognize a tendency for those of the same sex to become alienated, daughter from mother and son from father. The daughter sees in her mother the authority which imposes limits on her will, whose task it is to bring her to that renunciation of sexual freedom which society demands in certain cases. Mother is a rival who objects to being set aside. To the son, the father is the embodiment of the social compulsion to which he so unwillingly submits; the person who stands in the way of his following his own will of his early sexual pleasures and, when there is family property, his enjoyment of it. The relation between father and daughter and mother and son would seem less liable to disaster, the latter relation furnishes the purest examples of unchanging tenderness, undisturbed by any egoistic considerations. Therefore, there is nothing to wonder at if the dreams of a great number of people bring to light the wish for the death of their parents, especially of the parent whose sex is the same... We also find this death wish where there is no basis for it in real life and where the adult will never have to confess to entertaining it in his waking life. The reason for this is that the deepest and most common motive for estrangement, especially between parent and child of the same sex, came into play in the earliest years of childhood... The son, when quite a little child, already begins to develop a peculiar tenderness towards his mother; he looks upon her as his own property and regards his father as a rival who disputes his sole possession. Similarly, the little daughter sees in her mother as the one who disturbs her tender relation with her father and occupies a place she feels that she herself could very well fill.'

According to Freud, in the case of the boy, castration anxiety develops along with the Oedipus Complex. Because of his hostility towards his father he develops the fear that his genitals will be mutilated. Freud says, 'It is not at all uncommon for a little boy, who is beginning to play with his penis—and has not yet learnt that he must conceal such activities—to be threatened by parents or nurses that his member or his offending hand will be cut off. We are content to understand that the child concocts a threat of a kind out of his knowledge that autoerotic satisfactions are forbidden, on the basis of hints and allusions—whence comes the necessity for these phantasies, and the material for them? I believe that these primal phantasies are a phylogenetic possession. It seems quite possible to me that castration itself was in prehistoric periods of human family a reality.'

Corresponding to the said complex in the boy, the girl develops, what Freud describes as 'the deprivation complex'. She develops a feeling that, because of the absence of penis in her, she is deprived of something automatically. This feeling is associated with feelings of shame and resentment, which are generally repressed leading to the formation of deprivation complex. She feels that she has already been castrated for her sexual fantasies.

Infantile sexuality is repeated in adolescence in more or less the same proportion as in childhood. The oral phase of childhood may manifest itself in the form of nail biting, the anal sadistic stage by a noisy behaviour and an interest in the excretory function. The Oedipus situation becomes more prominent. Failure in the resolution of this complex may lead towards homosexual direction of the libido. This, according to Freud, is so because of narcissism, which impels the individual to favour the choice of a lover-object of his own sex rather than of the opposite sex. For the boy, such a situation is also favourable because this helps him to maintain his attachment with his mother. The narcissistic influence may persist even after the homosexual stage, but commonly it ends up with this homosexual phase. This narcissistic element has to do a good deal with the popular approval of the marriage. Where this narcissistic element is fully resolved, the prospects of stability of marriage are good. Another factor that counts in marriage is called anaclitic, which means dependence. This leads the boy to select a girl who takes care of him like a mother, or a girl to select a boy who protects her like a father. For example, a girl may select a boy who will protect either by size, status, wealth or ability. Similarly, a boy may choose a wife who, like his mother, sees that he lacks nothing. Many girls select husbands who correspond to their idea of masculinity or unresolved mating fear. This may make them select effeminate weaklings as husbands. The flow of the libido may end in one of the following ways:

(1) **Outward – to an object of love:** In such cases, the individual develops love for a member of the opposite sex, which is the normal development of the libido.

(2) **Inward – to self-love (narcissism):** Here, the libido is turned inward and is attached to the ego. This is called narcissism. Freud mentions a secondary form of narcissism, when the libido fails to find a lover object. The individual sets up the object as a fantasy within himself and proceeds to identify himself with that fantasy. To this mechanism, Freud applies the term 'introversion'. Narcissism develops as a normal phase of development. His creative achievement is determined by the extent of his success in detaching his libido from his ego.

(3) **Arrest – Fixation on an object (immature choice):** When the libido is detached from the ego, it seeks a love object to which it becomes attached. This attachment is called cathex and the object is said to be cathected. In the normal development, the first love-object is mother and the final one the mate. The libido may remain attached to an object at any point; for example, it may remain attached to mother.

When this love-object—on which fixation occurs—is the parent of the opposite sex, we have the Oedipus situation in the case of a boy, and Electra situation in the case of a girl.

(4) **Backward – Fixation on an object of earlier choice:** Regression means the attachment of the libido to a love-object belonging to an earlier stage in development. For example, a young man may fall in love with a girl but, when he is frustrated by the girl, he may fall back upon his earlier object of love, i.e., mother.

(5) **Dammed up – Unexpressed (repression):** When the person does not select an external love object, either the libido is attached to the ego or is repressed. In case of repression, it may go down into the unconscious.

(6) **Deflected – Into channels of social value (sublimated):** In the case of sublimation, the libido expresses itself in some such activity as is socially approved. Freud writes: 'We believe that civilization has been built up, under the pressure of the struggle for existence, by sacrifices in gratification of the primitive impulses and that it is to a great extent forever being recreated, as each individual successively joining the community repeats the sacrifice of his instinctive drive that is sublimated as the sex urge. In this case, the sex energy is turned aside from its sexual goal and diverted towards other

ends that are not sexual but socially more valuable. The process is difficult and there is a danger that rebellion of the sexual impulses may occur.'

Criticism of Psychoanalysis

Despite its immense appeal, psychoanalysis has met with strong opposition. Some going so far as to say that it is not a science at all. Many of the findings of psychoanalysis have been challenged by psychiatrists. We have seen that Freud traces most of the psychological troubles to an individual's early sexuality, especially during infancy. This sexuality during infancy has itself been challenged by some psychologists. Jung and Adler, Freud's students, tried to alter his teaching in this respect. The creative factor has been ignored in Freud's system of psychoanalysis. Freud admits that we can do nothing to change the factor of heredity. In his method of psychoanalysis Freud has merely dealt with Ego, Id and Superego, but has ignored the higher moral and spiritual side of human nature. Freud's extension of the term sex far beyond the commonly accepted usage has been highly criticized. There are many internal inconsistencies and obscurities. The Oedipus complex has been criticized a lot. Freud's new theory on the ego-trends points to a complex interplay between the ego and the libido, and to self-love which makes all this very confusing. The academic psychologists dislike a lack of directness in the Freudian statements. Figures of speech like censor, Oedipus complex, conflict, censorship, dream-work etc. appear to them quite out of place in a scientific world.

Other forms of treatment involve environmental manipulation stressing on improvement of the environment where the mental patients live.

Drug therapy has been currently used by psychiatrists successfully. There are other miscellaneous treatments such as surgical treatment, hydrotherapy, physical therapy, massage, whirlpool baths, therapeutic exercises, and imagery and daydream methods etc. These are all highly specialized techniques and should always be given by specialists.

Eastern Therapies

Yoga Therapy: In this method, mental conflicts, unpleasant urges and tendencies are cured through yogic methods. The method of yoga consists of eight steps: (i) *Yama*, i.e., abstention from violence, falsehood, dishonesty, sexual action and acquisitive tendencies; (ii) *Niyama*, which means observance of purity, contentment, austerity, self-study and resignation; (iii) *Asana* comprises certain physical postures; (iv) *Pranayama*, which involves developing control over breath; (v) *Prathyahara*, which means withdrawal of mind from objects; (vi) *Dharana*, which means concentration on the object of contemplation; (vii) *Dhyana*, which means focusing of mind on the object on one point; and (viii) *Samadhi*, which means continuous, uninterrupted focusing of mind on the object without the awareness of the self. Through yoga, mental distractions, unpleasant memories and thoughts, persecutions and obsessions fade away and subsequently die. Readers interested in yoga might refer books on the subject by masters like B.K.S. Iyengar.

Meditation and Zen Buddhism: The aim of this method is enlightenment. It involves sitting with a single mind. Dogan, the founder, says, 'Avoid distracting contacts and activities. Don't eat too much or too little. Sit in a quiet place on a thick rug or mat with a pillow under your seat and your legs crossed, in half or full lotus position, or sit in a straight-back chair, with your feet flat on the floor. With your back straight, breathe naturally from the depths of the lower part of the abdomen. Get concentrated, but not in thought'. Sitting, according to this method, is regarded as the gateway of truth to get liberation.

Author's Personality Theory

Decades of experience with the mentally ill, and exposure to various methods of cure all over the world, has prompted me to propose my own theory of personality, which is influenced by both Western and Eastern traditions. The Western psychologists, who have influenced me the most, in propounding this theory, are: Carl Jung, Freud, Gardner Murphy, B.F. Skinner, and Ken Wilbur. As far as the Eastern psychologists are concerned, there is no one particular psychologist but a host of them, most of them being yogis of India. The first one, with whom I was in touch during the years 1937-42, was Shri Akhand Swami of Gangotri. During the my lifetime, I not only met a number of yogis but also read a lot of literature on yoga; for example, *Yoga Therapy* by Swami Sivanand, *Hindu Psychology & Mental Health* by Swami Akhilanand (1948, 1952), *Yoga & Western Psychology* by Geraldine Coster, *Synthesis of Yoga* by Sri Aurobindo (1949, 54, 57), Mahesh Yogi on Transcendental Meditation, *Happiness – The TM Program Psychiatry & Enlightenment* by Bloomfield Harold H & Kory Robert B., *Sai Baba -The Holy Man & Psychiatrist, Spirit & The Mind; Sai Baba – Man of Miracles;* and *Autobiography of a Yogi* by Paramhansa Yogananda. It is with this background that I present this new personality theory.

The Main Principles of the Theory

Quantum of energy: The quantum of energy at a particular period of time is fixed for an individual but may change from time to time. (It can be increased with the help of yoga, meditation and psychoanalysis)—the physical and psychological energy being interchangeable to some extent, and also varying from individual to individual. Comparing it with the views of other personologists, Freud regarded the human organism as a complex energy system and he did not make any distinction between the energy that furnishes the power for breathing, digesting or other physiological functions and the energy that furnishes the power for thinking, remembering and other mental functions. Carl Jung has also expressed the same idea, though in a slightly different way, in the following words: 'The energy by which the work of the personality is performed is called psychic energy.' Jung uses the term 'libido' for this energy but, of course, he uses this term for life energy as well. Again, Jung does not take a positive stand on the relation of psychic energy to physical energy, but he believes that some kind of reciprocal action between the two is a tenable hypothesis.' Lewin, too, assumes that the person is a complex energy system. He says that the kind of energy that performs psychological work is called psychical energy but he does not relate psychical energy to other forms of energy. My observations of my patients, however, make me infer that there is an interchange of this energy not only between id, ego and superego systems but also between the physical system and the psychological functions. Of course, it was very difficult to measure this energy in quantitative terms. The only criteria used by me to measure this interchange of energy from physical to psychological function, and vice versa, were the behaviour patterns observed in different subjects in different situations; and the subjects were only those that I came across during my clinical practice. As the number of physical activities of such patients increased, a corresponding decrease was observed in the number of psychological activities, and vice versa. However, this phenomenon manifested itself at the later stages. In the earlier stages, both physical and psychological activities increased simultaneously. It was also observed that, up to a certain limit, the psychological activities increased or decreased in more or less direct proportion to the physical activities, although it has been difficult to define this limit. However, it was observed, this varies from individual to individual. Some individuals can go on increasing the two types of activities simultaneously to a greater limit than others, but then a limit is reached in every case. Beyond that, the increase in one type of activities adversely affects the other type of activities. It then happens that the two types of activities begin to have more or less inverse relationship. Again, this has a limit, varying from individual to individual, when one type of activities that is increasing, will not increase any more, and the second type of activities that is decreasing, will not decrease any more. This is perhaps nature's built-in mechanism to protect the individual from the breakdown of his physical and psychological systems.

Psychic energy at the conscious and unconscious levels: The total psychological energy is broadly distributed into two main domains – Conscious and Unconscious. The quantum in each keeps on changing from one to the other, keeping the total energy at a constant level in a given set of conditions. Freud's stand on this point is slightly different. He says that psychic energy is limited. It is distributed and used by id, ego and superego and there is always a competition among the three systems for the energy that is available. Jung, on the other hand, divides the unconscious into layers varying in depth and accessibility from personal unconscious to collective unconscious. His collective unconscious is a reservoir of a great fund of psychic energy held up in the form mostly of archetypes. They are the dynamic contents of the collective unconscious, but Jung has nowhere mentioned the energy relationships between various levels, i.e., from the conscious to the deepest layer of the collective unconscious. Aurobindo talks of the psychic energy at the conscious and unconscious levels. According to him, the psychic energy in the unconscious is always merging into the conscious in the process of evolution of human psyche, till the whole of the energy at the unconscious level is made conscious. This happens when the whole of the unconscious becomes conscious and, according to him, such a state is attained only by a fully illumined yogi. During my own observations of psychological cases, I noticed that a lot of conscious energy is depleted by conflicts, complexes and repressions etc. This energy is caught up in the unconscious, which otherwise would have been available at the conscious level. The individual needs a certain minimum of energy at the conscious level for adjustment to his environments. While treating my patients, I noticed that the maladjusted individuals immediately get adjusted when energy caught up due to certain conflicts, complexes and repressions was released from the unconscious or subconscious.

Neurosis and psychosis: Neurotic and psychotic symptoms made their appearances when the psychic energy at the conscious level falls below the minimum required for adjustment in a particular culture. This may be either due to the diversion of psychic energy to the unconscious or due to disorganization and dissipation of energy. The energy is diverted to the unconscious when conflicts, repressions take place and complexes are formed. The principle is in line with the thinking of personologists like Freud and Jung, except that the complexes as mentioned by Freud and Jung are not exactly the same in this culture, i.e., India. The manifestation of Oedipus Complex is a rare phenomenon. Money Complex is very common. In fact, I found money complex most common among the patients in India.

Unconscious to Conscious: The unconscious may be gradually made conscious to an extent, depending upon an individual's personal capacity and effort. The process, in a few cases, may ultimately lead to a state, what Aurobindo calls the superconscious state. The technique recommended by Indian yogis is that of meditation and self-analysis, whereas in the West, psychoanalysis, psychotherapy and psychosynthesis are quite popular for purging the psyche of the undesirable and unhealthy conflicts, complexes and repressions.

Sublimation: Beyond the heterosexual stage of development, there is a sublimated sexual or Divine stage, which only a few individuals may have attained.

Whereas Freud mentioned oral, anal, phallic, latent and genital stages of development, Sullivan delineated six stages in the development of personality, viz., (1) Infancy; (2) Childhood; (3) Juvenile Era; (4) Preadolescence; (5) Early Adolescence; and (6) Late Adolescence.

However, in my opinion the sublimated sex stage is the highest stage of development. This may be an idea borrowed from the eastern psychologists because most of the Western personologists stop short at the heterosexual stage, except Jung who mentions the ultimate goal as self-realization; or Kurt Goldstein who talks of self-actualization which he names as the sovereign purpose of life; or Abraham Maslow, whose meaning of self-actualisation relates to wholeness and unity of personality. During this last developmental stage, couples are generally faced with a number of problems., especially during the period when the process of sublimation is not complete. Sometimes, sexual tensions arise which result in serious consequences, such as marital discord, divorce, extra-marital relations, family quarrels and disruption of the families. Some persons try to overcome such problems through yoga therapy, different forms of meditations, by becoming members of *kirtan* (devotional songs) groups or seeking help from gurus (spiritual leaders). In the West, people seek help mostly through psychoanalysis, psychotherapy, psychosynthesis and recently through yoga and meditation as well. Another common problem faced by Indian couples during the transitional stage from heterosexual is that one partner may achieve sublimation earlier than the other. Such a situation may also become a source of trouble. Happy are the couples who achieve this sublimated sexual stage simultaneously.

Once complete sublimation has taken place, a person begins to feel complete and an integration results, which is highly cherished. He begins to identify himself with humanity at large and gets in touch with reality, which brings him wisdom of the highest order. For attaining complete sublimation, one has to have a sound philosophy of life, a high value system and a very disciplined life. The process, though simple, is beset with a number of difficulties especially if complications arise.

Fixation: Many of the human beings remain fixated at the heterosexual stage and some may even get fixated at an earlier stage of development. Such people mostly lead a miserable life and are often tense. They never enjoy the bliss of complete sublimation, which transforms one into a completely evolved person.

References

i. Akhilanand, Swami (1948), *Hindu Psychology: its Meaning for the West*, London, Routledge.

ii. Akhilanand, Swami (1952), *Mental Health and Hindu Psychology*, London, Allen & Unwin

iii. Aurobindo, Sri (1949), *Life Divine*, Aurobindo Ashram, Pondicherry.

iv. Aurobindo, Sri (1954), *Integral Yoga*, Aurobindo Ashram, Pondicherry.

v. Aurobindo, Sri (1957), *Synthesis of Yoga*, Aurobindo Ashram, Pondicherry.

vi. Dosajh, N.L. (1962), *Jung's Contributions to Psychoanalysis*, Darshana International, Vol. No. 2, pp. 85-87.

vii. Dosajh, N.L. (1963), *Yoga Philosophy & Western Psychology,* Darshana International, Vol. III, No.1, pp. 40-43.

viii. Dosajh, N.L. (1971), *Psychotherapy*, Sterling Publishers, New Delhi, pp. 75-137

ix. Dosajh, N.L. (1977), *Modification of Teacher Behaviour Through Microteaching,* Sterling Publishers, New Delhi.\

x. Dosajh, N.L. (1978), *'D' Test & Rorschach Test as Evaluation Tools In Treatment of Schizophrenic Patients*, Journal of Rajasthan Psychiatric Society, Vol. 1, pp. 28-35.

xi. Hall, Calvin S & Lindzey, Gardner (1978), *Theories of Personality*, John Wiley & Sons, New

York, Santa Carbara Chichester Brisbane, Toronto.pp.129.

xii.   Sivanand, Swami (1950), *Yoga in Daily Life*, Divine Life Society, Rishikesh.

xiii. Wilbur Ken, *The Ultimate State of Consciousness*, 1975-76.

xiv. Wilbur Ken, *The Spectrum of Consciousness,* Wsucator Quest, 1977.

xv. Wilbur Ken, *A Developmental View of Consciousness*, Journal of Transpersonal Psychology, Vol. II, No. 1, 1979.

xvi. Wilbur Ken, *No Boundary*, Los Angeles, Center Press, 1979 (new edition Shambala, 1981) Wilbur Ken, *The Atma Project*, Wsucator Quest, 1980.

Dr N.L. Dosajh

Development of Integrated Personality

When we think of integrated personality, we are talking of wholesome development—physical, emotional, social, mental and ethical—and all these aspects are properly balanced and integrated. The various aspects of personality are so interlinked that if one or more aspects of personality are weak, the process of complete integration suffers, resulting in a lopsided personality instead of a fully integrated one. A personality is integrated in a manner that it has no complexes, prejudices, phobias etc. Its value system is the one cherished by the human race all over the world. There are examples of such personalities all over the world and in every country, but the number is so small that they can be counted on fingers.

In this chapter, we wish to discuss a programme of education which is not meant for a few, but is applicable to all irrespective of caste, colour, creed, sex or nationality. Therefore, let us first try to understand what is personality before we can think of a programme of education for developing that personality. The chief characteristics of personality are:

i.   We can speak of personality only in case of adults, in children it is still taking shape.

ii.   Personality is entirely social. Its development takes place through social interaction. In fact, personality implies the reactions of others to one's own traits and actions.

iii. A personality is continually adjusting itself to its environment and to one's inner life.

iv. A personality is always trying to reach certain goals.

v. A personality functions as a unified whole.

Impact of Heredity and Environment

Individuals differ from each other because of differences in their heredity and environment. Heredity and environment are correlative factors in the development of personality. The former provides potentialities and the latter facilitates realisation of the potentialities. So, while studying personality, we have to take into consideration both the factors. The role of heredity and environment in the development of personality is an important factor. Heredity is important for the basic abilities a man possesses, such as intelligence, motor skills, activity of sense organs etc. Heredity is not very important for temperamental traits or emotional stability or for general activity. Heredity is least important in the formation of attitudes, beliefs and manners of thinking. These latter are formed through the impact of environments. For traits that are dependent upon anatomical features, heredity plays the maximum role and for the traits that are developed through training and education, the environments are more important than heredity. It is not a question of heredity versus environment but of heredity and environment determining the development of an individual. When an ovum is fertilised by a sperm, the genes of each are in interaction not only with each other but also with the surrounding liquid in the mother's womb. A change in the chemical nature of the surrounding liquid may totally change the structure of the developing embryo. So, at every stage, we find heredity traits interacting with surroundings, thus determining the next stage. All the while, intrinsic factors are interacting with the extrinsic ones. So, instead of debating whether one action of an individual is 'intrinsic' or 'learnt' it will be better to take it as a succession of stages, each stage being the result of interaction of the intrinsic with environmental factors.

In order to understand the process of integration of personality we may discuss it under the following heads:

1. Physical makeup of personality.
2. Emotional makeup of personality.
3. Social makeup of personality.
4. Mental makeup of personality.
5. Ethical makeup of personality.

Physical makeup of personality: In order to develop this aspect of personality it is important that the body should be well looked after. Some programme of physical exercise is important for this purpose. But some of the games, which arouse unhealthy competition and rivalry, not only may prove harmful to the physique of the individual but also may affect the personality development of the individual as a whole. As long as a game is played for game's sake, they are alright; but when they try to introduce an element of unhealthy competition, they become harmful. Again, a programme of physical exercise, when accompanied with music, proves beneficial both to the body and the mind. Yoga exercises can keep one young for a number of years; they keep one healthy and increase the lifespan. Where psychotherapy ends, yoga begins and leads to the integration of personality. These yoga exercises maintain physical balance; they tone up the endocrine glands, nervous and muscular systems. Most of the abdominal ailments can be cured with the help of specific yoga exercises. If these exercises are accompanied with pranayama, a person enjoys perfect physical health. Pranayam tones up the respiratory system.

Area of emotional makeup: Emotions have a great influence on behaviour pattern. Emotion is an affective experience and results from our inner adjustment. This experience results from mental and physiological stirred-up states in the individual. Emotions give richness and fullness to life, but if they overpower an individual, his behaviour may become irrational. In emotional growth, the child must be able to understand his own behaviour and that of the others. Therefore, emotional development takes place through training and understanding. Of course, physiological factors also are greatly responsible for the development of these emotions. The following are some of the causes, which hamper healthy development of emotions:

(i) **Fears and phobias:** Children are often taught to fear darkness, noises etc. Such fears are introduced just to control the child's behaviour, because fears seem to provide the easiest way for achieving this control. But these fears lay the foundations of a neurotic personality in the years to come. Phobias are morbid fears aroused by many situations such as dirt, crowds, heights, closed rooms, narrow and open places. Most of the phobias are traceable to feelings of guilt arising from sex transgressions, either real or imagined. For example, if a person meets with an unpleasant sex experience in a closed room, he is likely to develop a phobia for closed places. I had a case of claustrophobia who feared closed places because he used to masturbate in a closed room and then had a strong feeling of guilt. This feeling of guilt is the main cause for most of the phobias.

Fear cannot be totally done away with because, if intelligently used, it can be a strong constructive force in one's life, provided it is kept under control and is not abnormal. People, sometimes under the stress of fear, have worked wonders. Fear, as long as it spurs people to greater effort and useful work, is desirable but when it leads to abnormality, it is harmful. The best policy is to control fear rather than eliminate it altogether. Many situations which arouse fear should be met and conquered.

(ii) **Anxiety and worry:** A certain amount of concern about one's health, safety, plans and ideals etc. is necessary but if it is carried too far it is dangerous for the development of the individual and he may begin to suffer from anxiety neurosis. According to Carroll, the four principal characteristics of persons who suffer from anxiety neurosis are (1) morbid dread of the future; (2) indecision; (3) feeling of helplessness; and (4) resentment.

The morbid tendency that accompanies the anxiety state causes the individual to expect the worst. He is under great tension, irritable, uneasy, pessimistic and often panic-stricken.

According to Horney, 'There are four ways of escaping anxiety: rationalise it; deny it; narcotize it; avoid thoughts, feelings, impulses and situations which might arouse it.'

Everyone suffers from worry to a little or more extent. worry is transitory and disappears by the removal of the causal factors. Adolescents and young adults worry chiefly about vocational success, sex, health, finances etc. The author carried out a study of the adjustment problems of students. The results showed that most of the students felt maladjusted because of certain worries. Most of them showed financial worries. The other worries shown were about examination, ill-health of relatives, future career, studies, sex wife etc. Some of the peculiar worries were: 'To be one with the Universe, to ride to the stars etc.' In order to overcome worries and achieve adjustments the following measures are suggested:

1) A plan should be chalked out to meet the problem.
2) The problem to be faced should be thoroughly investigated and the information about it should be gathered from all possible sources.

3) The worry should be faced squarely by removing the cause as early as possible.

4) In order to remove serious worries, the cooperation of others should be sought.

Anger: Frustrations produce anger. When a person's plans are thwarted, he becomes angry. In the child, this anger is expressed in the form of screaming, kicking, stamping or sulking. In adults, it may be expressed in profanity, criticism, ridicule, backbiting or silence. Anger may help or harm an individual. It helps when it is provoked for a noble cause. For example, when it is aroused against an unscrupulous enemy of one's country, it makes one patriotic; but when one gets angry over trifles, one is likely to suffer both mentally and physically. In order to control the undesirable type of anger, one can change the stimulus that causes anger. A pleasant remark turns away anger. The best way is to substitute anger with love and affection.

Jealousy: It is a complex emotion that results from the feeling of subjugation, inferiority and fears. It also combines with it anger and the love of impulse. Jealousy is aroused when one fears that one will lose the much-desired affection of another person. Jealousy is aroused amongst children in a family or in a class, when the children find that their parents and teachers do not pay attention to them but to others. Those who get love and attention from their parents and teachers, become objects of jealousy.

The emotional life of an individual plays a very important part in maintaining his mental health. If emotional life is healthy, the chances of mental health improve. The healthy emotional life indicates that the person has an attitude of love and affection towards his near and dear ones. A person who is always picking up squabbles and quarrels with his relatives and friends is likely to suffer in his mental health.

Area of social makeup: Mental health of an individual is also dependent upon a good social group of friends. If the social group is imbued with good and noble ideas, the individual is likely to gain. In our religious books, great stress is laid upon the importance of *satsang*. The word 'satsang' means company of good people. In fact, an individual is a product of his social group. For the child, the first social group is his home and family life. Later, his social circle extends to the school. If the school is a good one, the child gains a lot, as far as his mental health is concerned. If the school provides opportunities for the proper expression of the child's drives, the child's mental health improves; however, if the drives are thwarted, ignored or otherwise suppressed, the child falls prey to emotional conflicts. With the passage of time, the child's social circle grows—the wider it is, the better for the individual, because humans need and desire association with other humans, especially if they are of the desirable type.

The following are some of the factors from the social makeup of an individual that create mental ill-health:

(i) **Bad company:** Most of the undesirable habits are picked up from the group of friends amongst whom an individual moves. Delinquent children can turn the normal children into delinquents. Formation of gangs results when delinquents form a group.

(ii) Improper development of social urge: Occasionally, the social instinct is not properly developed. The child, because of his introvertive tendency, prefers solitariness, which can result in mental ill-health. Such individuals fail to forge friendships easily and fail to develop this aspect of his personality.

(iii) Wrong attitudes: Sometimes, attitudes are formed which stand in the way of an individual's adjustment in new groups. Such a person cannot free himself from behaviour patterns of one group even though he desires acceptance as a member of another group. Thus, he experiences conflict in his new relationships.

(iv) Failure to attain socially acceptable behaviour in the satisfaction of a primitive urge: Such a situation generally results from fixed parental attitudes, prejudices, denials and shocks received during childhood, which get repressed and lead to the disassociation of the personality.

Area of mental makeup: If the mental drives of a person do not find expression, the possibilities of mental ailments increase. There must be avenues for self-expression, viz., speaking, writing or drawing etc. If such avenues are blocked, the individual is likely to become tense, which can make him fall a prey to mental troubles. Creative activities like art, painting, photography, modelling, composing verse, writing fiction etc. are excellent means for mental expression. A lifelong and absorbing hobby is essential for good mental health. People with no specific hobby find life dull, monotonous and aimless. Just as food is necessary for physical growth and upkeep, mental food is necessary for mental health. The habit of reading, writing—especially creative writing—and painting etc. help a lot in maintaining mental health.

Area of ethical makeup: From time immemorial, man has been waging a struggle against destructive forces. This struggle has been carried on in two directions from within and without. By means of scientific discoveries, man has been moulding natural forces to serve his ends. Physicists have probed into the secrets of the atom and have mastered an incalculable source of energy, which—if properly utilized—can transform the world into a heavenly abode. Researchers in the field of science and technology have enabled man to harness rivers, oceans and lakes. Even the highest of the mountain peaks have been scaled and the deepest of oceans explored. Geologists, through their research efforts, have pierced into the bowels of the earth. Efforts are afoot to conquer space, planets and stars. Day by day, researches are enabling man to conquer his environments. Natural forces like floods, volcanic eruptions, lightning, thunder and furies of weather—which in the past used to create awe and terror in the minds of men—have been more or less tamed and understood. Diseases like plague, smallpox, cholera, malaria etc., which used to take a heavy toll of life, have been nearly wiped off from the face of the earth. Though scientific research and discoveries have enabled conquering of many aspects of nature, still much remains to be explored and understood. With more discoveries happening regularly, man is acquiring greater control over his environments.

There is another direction in which man has been fighting his battle, i.e., the destructive forces from within. Animal urges in man also try to annihilate him. The crude urges like pugnacity, sex, hunger and power make man destroy other men. Efforts to conquer them and harness them, as in the case of external forces, have been made. Human nature itself is baffling, it has been challenging the human intellect for ages. Sages and saints, like scientists, have been engaged in the task of understanding nature and trying to modify it for the good of human race. There have been pioneers in this field who experimented on their own lives and conquered these animal urges, and then paved the way for others by setting personal examples. Since they happened to live in different environments, these pioneers worked out different plans for conquering the animal within man. Although their techniques were different, their purpose was the same—that of conquering oneself from within, that of overcoming the beast in man. These techniques or disciplines, as advocated by these pioneers, gave rise to different religions on the face of the earth. Krishna, Buddha, Mahavira, Jesus Christ, Prophet Mohammad, Guru Nanak, and others were some of the pioneers in this field. Different religions came into being to enable man to understand his true nature, to enable him transform the beast in him into nobler elements and to enable him to satisfy his craving to see the Unseen. People follow these religions, these disciplines, and realise their true nature; however, they get stuck upon the dogmas and rituals advocated by their religions. Such persons not only become a danger to themselves but also to the society at large. They become fanatics, megalomaniacs and tyrants, and become a source of potential danger. They are the persons who exploit religion for nefarious and selfish ends. Instead of inculcating love between man and man, they sow seeds of hatred and cause wars in the name of religion.

Although different religions appear to be different, on a closer analysis we find them to be fundamentally the same. In fact, they all converge to the same point and serve the same purpose—helping man to transform his animal nature into something higher and nobler. If the forms of various religions and disciplines differ, it is because the leaders of those religions were born and bred in conditions that were different geographically as well as culturally. The various religions may be compared to different paths leading to same peak of a mountain. The peak is the spiritual in man, and to reach it one may follow any path or religion or discipline according to one's temperament and convenience. One may not follow any of the existing religions, instead he may carve out a new discipline to attain the goal. It is just like a person carving out a new path to reach the peak of the mount. One may not like to tread the beaten track. Such a person requires more stamina and insight because dangers and pitfalls on a new path are many. For a common man, religions provide easy roads to achieve the best in him. When people reach the peak's summit through one religion or other, they feel and think alike. Their views are nearly the same. They become truly spiritual. Such persons are truly integrated personalities and are always sought out, loved and respected.

Man, in order to overcome the beast within, does need a religion or a discipline, more so in this fast-changing scientific age, when scientific researches are providing us with the processes and products that could be useful or harmful, depending upon their usage. The beast in man is likely to be a source of danger to human race. So, it is important that the beast in man must be made godlike so that security of human race is ensured. At least, the destiny of human race should be in the hands of men who have transformed their animalism into spiritualism through any religion or discipline. This much is certain that man does need a religion or a discipline for his own security and the security of his race. Now, the question arises as to what should be the shape of these religions or disciplines? Today, man is developing a scientific outlook towards his environments. He looks upon the old religions with scepticism because their teachings are mostly dogmatic and based on blind faith. Dogmatic teachings do not appeal to the modern scientific mind. Unless these old religions do away with dogmatism, they are likely to disappear gradually. The modern man is looking for a religion grounded in scientific temper and principles. In this age of real-time communications, fast transport and extremely busy lifestyle, the old-style time-consuming religious rituals and ceremonies are becoming a big hinderance, even irrelevant. Either these rituals and ceremonies should be simplified or they will fade away. If the religions die, there is always a risk of man devoid of religion, who would be dangerous not only to himself but also to the entire human race. To be without religion-based ethics and morality is like being a rudderless boat. The argument, that one can be grounded in higher ethical and moral principles without any religion, holds true only in rare cases. The common man needs a religion. Therefore, an ideal solution would be to simplify the religions of the world and base them on scientific principles. This will go a long way in maintaining the mental health of the people.

A proper integration of the above areas

Mental ill health can also arise if the said five areas are not properly integrated. When any one or more of the said areas grow out of proportion, it might lead to mental ill-health. For example, if a great scholar makes progress in his intellectual life at the cost of his emotional and social life, one day he might find himself maladjusted in society, resulting in his mental ill-health.

Some of the techniques that are employed by persons to maintain mental health are as follows:

(a) **Rationalisation:** People try to justify their erratic behaviour by trying to give justification which, at first sight, appears reasonable but are generally afterthoughts. Although these reasons are generally half-truths, they help the individuals maintain mental health. These individuals do not consciously lie or attempt to deceive; they simply express their attitudes towards what they have done. This process of self-justification is called rationalisation. At times, everyone resorts to rationalisation. If it becomes habitual, it is a serious sign of mental ill-health.

(b) **Daydreaming:** Daydreaming is thinking of future imaginatively and taking pleasure in one's imaginary successes. Occasionally, even normal people daydream. But, if resorted to frequently, it becomes a serious threat to mental health. Such a situation arises when a person repeatedly meets with failures. The individual withdraws and starts living in a world of dreams and begins to derive imaginary pleasures.

(c) **Hysteria:** In hysteria, the person tries to escape from unpleasant situations by showing symptoms of physical or mental disability, which have absolutely no organic bases. In hysteria, the person may show signs of blindness, paralysis, headaches, stomach aches etc. The causes of such troubles are emotional. A hysterical person differs from the malingerer because the former really behaves in a way that he shows he has the trouble while the latter merely pretends.

(d) Projection: In this mechanism, the individual refers to other individuals' faults, which are actually his own.

(e) Identification: In this mechanism, the individual imagines himself to be undergoing the experiences of another person. Such a phenomenon is very common when we see a movie. People generally identify themselves with a heroic character and experience the joys and sorrows of that character in the movie.

(f) Regression: In this mode of adjustment, the individual returns to his earlier modes of behaviour when he finds that he has failed to face a particular situation.

(g) Negativism: In this mechanism, the individual refuses to obey commands or requests and has the tendency to do the opposite. This attitude develops as a result of frustrations. Such individuals refuse to attack the problem facing them. They become stubborn, contradictory and rebellious. They are likely to develop uncooperative and negativistic behaviour.

(h) Sympathy: In this mode of adjustive reaction, the individual avoids solving his problems by obtaining the sympathy of others. The individual tries to gain attention and secure expression of concern over his difficulties.

(i) Compensation: According to Crow & Crow, compensation may be defined as the utilization of extra energy in the development of a trait or traits to alleviate the tensions caused by a real or imagined defect. For example, a stutterer might compensate his defect to such an extent that he may become a great orator. In transferred compensations, the individual becomes overactive in some functions which is other than the one of his deficiencies. For example, a student who is not good at studies may compensate by excelling in games and athletics, thus attracting public attention.

(j) Depersonalisation: In this type of defence mechanism, everything appears unreal to the person. Even his own body appears alienated. It is a sort of escape mechanism from a difficult situation—perhaps, a severe conflict.

Some types of compensations are harmful. For example, an individual may overcompensate for his physical, mental, social or economic inferiority, and may begin to pretend superiority without any basis. Bullying, blustering, and trying to show off etc. are compensations of this type. Compensation mechanism is useful to an individual if it takes the shape of socially approved substitute goals. Under tense and frustrating situations, an individual may employ any one or more of the said mechanisms for adjustment. These mechanisms represent an unconscious attempt on the part of an individual to solve his problems and preserve the integrity of his personality.

Dr N.L. Dosajh

Modification of the Basic Nature of Man

The basic nature of man, which constitutes innate urges, needs to be modified a little, as some of these urges in their crude form are harmful both to the individual and the society. The process of modification can be brought about through education and training. Basic urges can be modified in a number of ways. If the process is sound, the individual's personality improves and the society stands to benefit, and if the process is unsound both the individual and the society suffer.

Our animal urges need to be modified into something nobler and higher. Our fundamental personality pattern may be considered to be constituted of physical, emotional, social, mental and spiritual. Through a programme of physical exercises, the development of all the parts of one's body can be ensured. Various sports, games and exercises have been useful in this aspect. But the most important thing to be taken note of is that the development of all the parts takes place harmoniously. No part should be neglected at the cost of another. There are cases on record where a lopsided development of the body has resulted in harming health at a later stage. Mere development of strong muscles, say of legs or arms, is not enough. What is desired is that all muscles and parts of the body should be so developed that there is general toning up of the whole body. A suitable programme of sports and games, coupled with yogic exercises, should go a long way in achieving this goal. The entire programme should be geared up for the development of a supple, active body with a constitution that is not rigid but flexible.

For the modification of crude emotions, more is caught rather than taught. A congenial atmosphere, both at home and outside, goes a long way in bringing about the desired change. The processes involved in the modification of the basic nature of man are repression, inhibition, redirection, sublimation and catharsis.

1. **Repression:** Certain behaviours of a child can be antisocial and immoral. Unless such behaviours are checked, society will go to pieces. For example, the acquisitive instinct of an individual may make him snatch away the things that do not belong to him. One of the ways of checking such a tendency is to repress it, i.e., such tendencies are not allowed to function freely. Whenever such tendencies become active, they are repressed. This is not a desirable method of modification of instincts because here the instinctive energy is not utilised but repressed and thus lost. This repression, if carried too far, has a deleterious effect on the unconscious of the individual. The energy behind these instincts is damped down into the unconscious and, when the repression is carried too far, it may result in the breaking down of the individual's personality. Such an individual will revolt against the society and will lose his mental equilibrium. Therefore, extreme

repression should be avoided. If the instinctive tendencies are repressed, it may make the individual to satisfy those repressed instincts in manners that are antisocial and immoral. Therefore, repression is generally harmful. A person who is repressed often, generally fails to grow. His faculties remain undeveloped. In a real-life situation, a certain amount of repression is necessary but then the teachers and elders must know the limits. For example, the sex urge, if allowed to have its own way, would create chaos and confusion in the society. Therefore, sometimes, it becomes essential to repress this urge to some extent. The child should be trained to exercise this restraint by himself. However, the elders should ensure that this process is not taken to the extreme. Sex urge can find satisfaction in a sublimated form. The children of two sexes can participate in useful activities like games, sports and hobbies etc., together.

2. **Inhibition:** By inhibition, we mean the controlling of the emotions. There are occasions when the expression of certain emotions is not healthy, and the occasion demands that we control our emotions. If we can control them, then we say the emotions have been inhibited. Suppose, an employee finds something funny in his superior's actions or words and feels like laughing at him but knows that it would annoy the superior and so, controls himself; this is inhibition. The ability to inhibit emotions is an

important quality that one acquires through training and experience. Therefore, sometimes, a child has to be trained to inhibit emotions. Although desirable, such inhibition of emotions should never be taken to extremes. If a child inhibits emotions all the time, he might become a victim of all sorts of tensions. If the level of such tensions gets too high it may result in nervous breakdown. So, while the child should be able to inhibit emotions when necessary, he should be able to express them freely when the occasion demands. Children, who are inhibited too much, fail to grow. Their personality development is interfered with and some of them end up suffering psychological problems. It must be stressed that the training in inhibiting emotions rarely comes through lecturing and advising. It is mostly through a process of unconscious imitation. For a healthy development of emotions, a number of occasions should also be provided for children to express their emotions freely. In fact, such occasion should interpose the occasions demanding inhibition of emotions.

3. **Redirection:** Redirection of emotions is desirable, especially when a particular direction for their expression is blocked. The emotions, when aroused, are like a river in spate. One cannot block the flow of water, but can certainly redirect its flow into different channels and thus have a control over it. In fact, one of the best methods in preventing a river in flood from causing damage to surrounding areas is to

divert its overflow into side channels. An educationist has to create adequate means for expression of emotions. Music, poetry, dance, drama, games and sports etc. are some of the useful means for the redirection of emotions. Emotions, when blocked or ill-directed, lead to damage. Most of the acts of aggression, indiscipline or violence are the result of improper direction and emotional conflict. Redirection provides a healthy means for the control of an individual's aggressive behaviour. Lack of understanding of this basic fact results in great harm to the society. In a brilliant article, *On War and Peace in Animals and Man*, appearing in 'Science' (a publication of the American Association for the Advancement of Science), Dr Tinbergen of the University of Oxford asks, 'Can education produce non-aggressive men?' and concludes, 'Elimination through education of the internal urge to fight will turn out to be very difficult, if not impossible.' Dr Tinbergen forgets that this urge to fight can be easily redirected into useful channels. Of course, education cannot produce a totally non-aggressive man but it can certainly produce a man whose aggression is directed into useful channels. And, that is exactly the aim of education. Bhakti is one of the useful methods of redirection of emotions. This method has been prevalent in India for ages.

4. **Sublimation:** Sublimation is the process of transformation of animal nature of man into

something nobler and ethical. The basic urges, through a process of education and training, get transformed into higher values of life. The process is difficult and takes a long time for complete sublimation. Temporary sublimation may be achieved earlier but, in such a case, the chances of regression to earlier modes of behaviour are immense. According to Western psychologists, complete and permanent sublimation of basic urges is an impossibility and assert that only partial sublimation can be achieved. All degrees of sublimation can be found between these two extremes. The extent of an individual's ability to transform his basic urges into higher values of life depends upon a number of constitutional and environmental factors. Eastern sages like Patanjali and Swami Dayanand provide yogic method for the complete transformation of basic urges into higher values of life.

It is possible to achieve the modification of basic urges into corresponding sentiments of patriotism, friendship, truth, beauty and health etc. through cultural activities, social gatherings, religious activities, study of arts and sciences and physical activities. A harmonious development of these leads to integration whereas a lopsided development results in the formation of negative traits like parochialism, bigotry etc. Participation in the cultural activities of one's own culture develops the sentiment of patriotism. Participation in the cultural activities of other cultures develops an attitude of appreciation for other cultures. This is normal development. But too much or obsessive participation in the activities of one's own culture only might result in fanaticism. Similarly, participation in various social groups may lead ultimately to the formation of a sentiment of friendship but participation in the activities of a particular group to the exclusion of other groups may lead to the formation of the trait known as groupism. Such a person works for the good of his own group and may even try to harm the interests of other groups. On the other hand, a person, while being a member of a particular group, participates in the activities of other groups and appreciates their good activities succeeds in the formation of the sentiment of friendship. Religious activities like community prayer, community dancing etc. are meant to satisfy the spiritual urge in man and lead to the formation of a sentiment for higher values of life. But the reverse is also true. This urge may get distorted and the person may become a fanatic. The malformation takes place when the person ignores the substance but chases the shadow, for the purpose behind them. The study of the arts and sciences provides satisfaction to a sentiment for beauty and truth. But when the individual merely crams the facts from books on arts and sciences without understanding them, he may become pedantic. Lastly, different kinds of physical activities, like games, sports, rhythmic exercises etc., help the physical growth and develop a sentiment for health which ensures freedom from disease and longevity. On the other hand, concentration on one type of sport or athletic item may lead to only a lopsided development that may not necessarily result in good health and longevity. For example, a weightlifter, in order to compete in weightlifting tournament, may over-exercise his arm muscles which may result in the breakdown of his health in the long run.

The sentiments thus formed may get organised into several sentiment-complexes or a 'master-sentiment', which has been named by McDougall as the sentiment of self-regard. The formation of sentiments takes place as a result of the following processes:

1. Imitation
2. Sympathy
3. Suggestion

McDougall and his followers are of the view that 'Imitation' and 'Sympathy' begin to appear during early infancy. 'Suggestion' begins a little later. In fact, these three processes go on throughout life and are mainly responsible for the modification of basic urges. A good educationist makes use of all these processes for the formation of the sentiments.

Imitation: Imitation is very common both among animals and man. Animals like sheep—that herd together—imitate one another blindly. A child imitates its elders. There are two types of imitation, viz., conscious and unconscious. In conscious imitation, the child deliberately imitates the model that it admires. He may copy his teacher's pronunciation. In unconscious imitation, no deliberate attempt is made, but certain things pass on unconsciously, for example, mannerisms in a family. Imitation of good examples should be encouraged among children. The teacher's own personality is very important because most children copy their teacher's personality unconsciously. Similarly, the personality of parents has a profound effect on their children.

Sympathy: Instances of sympathy are sympathetic anger, sympathetic laughter, sympathetic tears and these can be seen in cinema halls. The opposite of sympathy is antipathy. A good teacher always has an attitude of sympathy towards his pupils. In turn, this generates an attitude of sympathy in the pupils. The reverse is quite dangerous for the teachers as well as for the students. If a teacher has an attitude of antipathy towards his students, the students are likely to develop an attitude of antipathy not only towards that teacher but also towards the subject he teaches. This is called transference. In an experience of sympathetic emotion, the person experiences sympathetic emotions. The person may feel that others have the same emotions, tendencies and wish objects as himself. This is named as projection. In another situation, the person may identify his own wishes and emotions with others. This is called introjection. "When we appreciate others' emotions or desires, since they follow the lines of those stages that we have passed, then our experience is that of introjection." When we "feel ourselves into" other objects, this is called empathy. Our appreciation of art is directly proportional to the degree of empathy possible for us with the painting, sculpture, scenery or any other piece of art before us.

Sympathy is common in teacher-student relationship. The emotions of the teacher, through the process of sympathy, unconsciously pass on to the students. So, before a teacher is actually allowed to enter his profession it is essential that all abnormalities are removed. Otherwise he may prove to be a source of danger to his students. Teachers, who are sportsmen, virtuous, honest, truthful and patriotic, pass on these traits to their students through the process of unconscious sympathy. On the other hand, teachers who are fanatics turn their students into fanatics too. In fact, such traits are caught rather than taught through the process of unconscious sympathy.

Suggestion: This is a process in which a student unquestioningly accepts the accuracy of facts presented by the teacher. This will happen only if the teacher is known for his honesty and integrity. The statements that he makes are free from contradictions. Also, he is an authority in his subject. The suggestion is accepted only if there is a rapport between the teacher and the students. Sometimes, the suggestion works negatively. This happens when the person to whom the suggestion is given is contra-suggestible. Such a person, when asked to do a particular thing, does the opposite. The best is to see that the adolescents do not become contra-suggestible. If they, perchance, develop this perverse habit, they should be handled psychologically.

The above three processes of imitation, sympathy and suggestion, if used intelligently, can help the educators a lot in modifying the behaviour of individuals. The basic urges get modified into sentiments which, in the process of modification, get organised into a whole set of sentiments designated as 'character'.

The term 'character' is very wide and technically has a place in Ethics. What we see in the case of an individual in his 'conduct' and we judge his character from its expression in conduct. Again, character is with reference to a certain code of ethics laid down by society. As long as a person acts according to the codes of ethics laid down by the society, we designate him as a man of character.

There are other techniques of altering human behaviour, which are commonly used in the case of psychological patients. Some of them are as under:

1. Psychotherapy, Behaviour Therapy and Sophrotherapy
2. Hypnosis
3. Use of drugs and Mystic Practices
4. Sensory and Social Isolation

Psychotherapy, Behaviour Therapy & Sophrotherapy: Behaviour therapy is a multiplicity of psychological techniques for the treatment of behaviour related problems. Three of them are very important: psychoanalytic, client-centred and existential. In psychoanalytic therapy, the patient is gradually made to understand his problems under the active guidance of a therapist. The therapist uses various types of techniques like free association, dream analysis, projective techniques etc. to understand and interpret the unconscious and repressed desires, conflicts and guilt feelings of the patient. In client-centred therapy, the patient tries to integrate his personality through the insight that he gains into his problems with the help of the therapist. In turn, the therapist provides a permissive atmosphere and an attitude of acceptance and encourages the patient to give free expression to his repressed feelings; he lets the patient's repressed emotions to come up on the surface. In existential therapy, the patient—through communications and relatedness with therapist—becomes aware of his problems and takes the responsibility of making certain choices and taking certain decisions so as to face such challenges of his life as are in existence. He begins to take his existence seriously and responsibly. In all the above techniques, insight into one's own problems play an important role in the process of cure. That is why these have been designated as insight therapy.

Besides these, we have what we call behaviour therapy, in which the therapist produces some definite changes in the habits and actions of the patient. In behaviour therapy, various technological gadgets may also be brought into service. For example, behaviour therapy in a closed-circuit television studio—where feedback to the patient of his faulty behaviour is provided—has been found to be far more effective and quicker than otherwise. Whereas insight therapies increase the understanding of the patient of himself, the behaviour therapies eradicate the symptoms of the patient without much concern regarding their origin and meaning. Unlike insight therapists, behaviour therapists do not take therapy as a process for promoting insight but as a manipulated and controlled procedure for modifying and changing the symptoms of behaviour disorder, not bothering themselves at all about possible self-understanding (Eysenck, 1960).

Another type of psychotherapy, which has come into use recently, is known as sophrotherapy. It is a blend of Western psychology and Indian spirituality. It balances the concepts and techniques of the West with a contemplative awareness of the East. Dr Alfonso Caycedo of Columbia (South America) founded it and named it Sophrology. In his technique, change in the consciousness of the patient is of fundamental importance.

Hypnosis: It is instrumental in altering certain modes of behaviour. Although direct suggestion is useful in many cases, it is found that sensory conditioning under hypnosis is more effective. But it may be clearly understood that hypnosis is not an occult state but a form of social interaction.

1. **Use of drugs & mystic practices:** Drugs, particularly those known as psychedelic drugs, have been used to decrease anxiety, emotional disturbance, reactions and also to control and remove many other more severe symptoms. Additionally, they have been used to expand and enhance the awareness of felt and perceived experiences. In fact, a new science — known as psychopharmacology —

has developed as a behaviour science discipline as a result of man's improved knowledge of the effects of different drugs. Drugs are currently classified into four main categories according to their chemical effects, viz., tranquilisers, anti-depressants, non-barbiturate sedatives and psychotomimetic or psychedelics. The drugs of the first type are used to calm psychiatric patients, the second to stimulate activity, the third to reduce activity, induce sleep, while the fourth to produce drastic changes in the psychological state of the individual. Some of such drugs are mescaline, a product of hemp or marijuana; psilocybin, extracted from mushroom; and peyote cactus; LSD (lysergic acid diethylamide) derived from a natural product called ergot—a fungus that grows on rye.

(i) **Creative effect:** It has been observed in several studies that both creative activity and the states induced by psychedelic drugs have the following features in common: (a) low degree of psychological defensiveness, lack of rigidity, tolerance for ambiguity, tendency to receive and integrate apparently conflicting information, sensitive awareness of feelings, and openness to all phases of experience; (b) evaluation being based primarily not on outside standards and prejudices but on one's own feelings, intuition and aesthetic sensibility; (c) the ability to toy with ideas, colours, shapes and hypotheses, to think in terms of analogues and metaphors; (d) the ability to feel spontaneity and freedom. Opium, cocaine, hashish, mescaline and LSD belong to this class of drugs.

(ii) **Cognitive effect:** Small dosage of psychedelic drug renders the subject capable of "thinking unusually sharply, quickly and clearly." Here, new dimensions of ideas and objects seem to emerge having novel interrelationships, all viewed at once.

(iii) **Psychotic effect:** When a psychedelic drug is administered to a subject who does not know what to expect or how to respond, he tends to develop paranoid delusions, delusions of reference, disorientation and confusion, panic and an extreme feeling of isolation – these may well be labelled as psychotic. If non-psychotic experiences are desired, the subject has to be prepared for that; he must feel secure in a friendly atmosphere, he must be willing to accept a reality which is very different from the usual reality, and so on.

(iv) **Therapeutic effect:** The material that was unconscious and repressed becomes vividly conscious. This leads to abreaction and catharsis, which may be utilised for diagnostic and therapeutic purposes. Many investigators have pointed out that, under the effect of psychedelic drugs, suggestion seems to play an important role because the patients under the Freudian therapy tend to regress to infancy and early childhood, recalling incidents from the various stages of psychosexual development, whereas archetype symbols are expressed by patients under the Jungian therapy.

(v) Aesthetic effect: Another type of psychedelic experience is a kaleidoscopic perception of form, colour and sound. Fascinating changes in sensation and perception occur. Sound becomes visible, objects become alive, ordinary things become imbued with great beauty, forms become more vivid, colours grow richer and deeper. One feels as if one has entered into a magnificent atmosphere of art and beauty—the Paradise. Perhaps, it is this experience of enhanced sensations and their aesthetically pleasing blending that attracts many people to take psychedelic drugs.

(vi) Mystic effect: Under certain conditions, feelings of awe and reference are evoked, which is termed as transcendental or mystical experience. In an experimental content, Phanke analysed the reported mystic experience induced by LSD, and comparing the various dimensions of this consciousness with those recorded in literature of spontaneously occurring mystical experience, he found that there was a close affinity between the two. Both comprise, among other experiences, (a) a feeling of unity or oneness, in which the subject-object dichotomy vanishes; (b) transcendence of time and place; (c) deeply experienced feeling of love, peace, joy and wonder; (d) a feeling of insight and illumination pertaining not so much to facts as to a sense of values; (e) paradoxicality; and (f) transience.

Sensory and social isolation: Reports of prisoners in solitary confinement, explorers and shipwrecked sailors as well as mystics and subjects exposed to experimental isolation show that the ability to think and reason suffers, perception gets distorted, feeling states are grossly disturbed, imagery becomes extraordinarily vivid, which sometimes take the form of bizarre hallucination and delusion. Sensory and social deprivation is conducive to what Kris calls 'regression in the service of the ego', a mechanism by which scientists, poets, artists, intellectuals and other creative workers can allow themselves regressive fantasies in order to use such material more constructively.

Yoga and meditation: These techniques are extremely useful as modifiers of behaviour. However, these must be learnt under the guidance of a competent teacher.

Aetiology of Mental Disorders

Mental disorders are generally caused not by just one aetiological factor alone but many factors which may be divided into two main categories: predisposing and precipitating. The predisposing factors may be hereditary, physiological, while precipitating factors may owe their existence to toxins, bodily diseases, exhaustion and traumas. Sometimes, the predisposing factors alone may bring about a mental disorder, but often the predisposing factors may remain dormant until something from the environment acts as a precipitating cause.

Predisposing Factors

Heredity

How far heredity is responsible for causing mental disorders, is a hotly debated question and is very difficult to settle. It is just possible that heredity may not play a major role, and certain mental disorders may be a result of faulty upbringing and unfavourable environmental conditions. At the same time, data has been collected to study the role of heredity in the causation of mental disorders. Some results are presented below:

(a) Manic-depressive insanity has the greatest inherited taint.

(b) Schizophrenia has inherited abnormalities in about half the number of cases. The inheritance of this psychosis is usually dissimilar.

(c) Epilepsy has an inherited taint in 80 percent of cases. The transmission is frequently direct.

(d) A very high proportion of the forebears of mental defectives are alcoholics or the subjects of nervous diseases.

(e) Mother-to-daughter is one of the most common form of transmission.

Physiological: During puberty, adolescence, pregnancy and climacterium, the individual undergoes a physiological stress. As a result of this stress, the individual may become vulnerable to psychological troubles.

Age: Most of the mental disorders occur between the ages of 30 and 40 in males, and between the ages of 25 and 35 in females. General paresis is most common between 30 and 40 years. Dementia praecox occurs most commonly from 20 to 30 years, and manic-depressive is most likely to occur between 20 and 30 years.

Sex: Mental disorders are as common in men as in women. The unmarried are more prone to psychoses than the married ones.

Race: According to Kirby, dementia praecox, manic-depressive psychosis and other constitutional disorders are more common in the Jews than in others. The disorders owing to alcoholism are more common among the Irish people. General paresis occurs frequently amongst the Germans. Cases of psychosis are very common in people of African descent. Epilepsy is very common among Italians.

Personality: Personalities designated as introverted by Jung, schizoid by Kretschmer, shut-in by Hoch, tender-minded by James, Apollonians by Nietzsche, the devouring by Blake, vagotonic by Eppinger and Hess, are generally susceptible to schizophrenia. Personalities that are designated as extroverted by Jung, cycloid by Kretschmer, tough-minded by James, prolific-type by Blake, sympatheticotorics by Eppinger, and Dionysians by Nietzsche, generally suffer from manic-depressive psychosis.

Bodily types: Kretschmer's dysplastic or asthenic types are prone to suffer from schizophrenia. His pyknic type is prone to suffer from manic-depressive psychosis.

Endocrine types: The hyperthyroid types are likely to be irritable and excessively emotional. In the subthyroid type, retardation and memory impairment are common. Adrenal types may become neurasthenics. The pituitary types are prone to acromegaly—abnormal enlargement of limbs. They may also suffer from Frohlich's Syndrome.

Precipitating factors

The following are some of the factors that precipitate the onset of mental troubles:

a. **Frustrations:** Repeated frustrations exacerbate mental conditions. In individuals, having predisposing factors, frustrations make the libido regress to earlier levels of behaviour. If this process continues, the individual may become a victim of psychosis, like schizophrenia. In its extreme form, the individual simply rolls up, buries his head between his knees and assumes the foetal position.

This is an extreme form of regression and the individual, in this state, gets a false sense of security—like the one he had in his mother's womb.

b. **Physical illness:** A long, continued illness may become a major factor contributing to mental illnesses. Tuberculosis, heart troubles, tumours, pellagra, diabetes, gout, rheumatism, enlarged prostrate, arteriosclerosis etc. can become the precipitating factors.

c. **General weakness and exhaustion:** This results in fatigue and may produce toxins in the body. When an emotional trauma causes fatigue, it lets loose repressed complexes leading to mental disorder.

d. **Traumatic experiences:** Trauma generally results in traumatic psycho-neurosis or severe cases of traumatic psychoses. For example, head injuries can lead to traumatic psychosis.

e. **Emotional shocks:** Such emotional shocks as death of a near and dear one may also result in mental disorder.

f. **Toxins:** Toxins are of three kinds, viz., (i) Poisons like alcohol, opium, cocaine, mercury, lead, arsenic, carbon monoxide etc. (ii) Toxins resulting from diseases like syphilis, tuberculosis, typhoid, influenza and malaria etc. (iii) Endogenous toxins, which are produced within the body, e.g., focal sepsis, disorders of the thyroid etc.

Alcohol can cause mental disorders but alcohol in small quantities is a food. However, in large quantities, it is a narcotic. In a small quantity, alcohol could give relief from psychological stress. But, in excess, it is a symptom of mental disorder rather than a cause.

Syphilis, when inherited from parents, may give rise to juvenile G.P.I. cerebral psychosis etc. When syphilis is acquired, it may give rise to general paresis, cerebrospinal syphilis, tabes, arteriosclerosis etc. The knowledge of being exposed to syphilis may cause syphilophobia.

Dr N.L. Dosajh

Psychoneurosis: Classification and General Symptoms

The basic difference between psychosis and psychoneurosis is that the former is a major mental disorder whereas the latter is a minor one. In the former case, the contact of the individual with the realities of life is completely broken, but in the latter case, it is not broken although the subject displays an unusual behaviour. As such, by psychoneurosis we understand the minor abnormalities of the cognitive, emotional and motor processes, which usually only partially incapacitate the individual.

These minor deviations of personality are generally socially conditioned. The many reactions we may call neurotic in our culture and society, may well be considered quite normal in other cultures and societies. Similarly, the behaviour types that we consider quite normal may be considered neurotic in other cultures. Therefore, a person is considered psychoneurotic if, because of anxiety, he deviates from the norms accepted by his culture.

General symptoms

Although specific symptoms of the neurotic may vary widely, they have a number of personality characteristics in common, stemming from immaturities, weaknesses and incorrect evaluation of themselves. Some of the general symptoms are:

i) **Low stress tolerance:** The neurotic has a feeling of inadequacy and is unable to face the stress and strains of life. Consequently, he perceives many situations as threatening which would not be so perceived by normal persons. However, the neurotic may show exaggerated independence in which he refuses help.

ii) **Anxiety:** Anxiety is a pervasive factor underlying all neuroses. Sometimes, the anxiety is felt acutely, as in anxiety attacks but, more typically, the neurotic develops various defences for reducing the anxiety.

iii) **Emotional over-responsiveness:** Guilford pointed out that the characteristics shown by a neurotic can be called *neurotic emotionality* and *neurotic hostility*. These terms refer to the neurotics' over-responsiveness to minor irritations, and to their tendency to have a hostile and suspicious attitude towards the world they view as dangerous and threatening. They deal with their problems emotionally rather than rationally.

iv) **Lack of integrated behaviour:** As the neurotic cannot cope with stressful situations, he experiences anxiety. His behaviour becomes non-integrative. The neurotic's defences, though self-defeating, tend to be self-perpetuating because they appear to reduce his anxiety. If his defences are somehow weakened or eliminated, the anxiety returns.

v) **Rigidity in behaviour:** The neurotic does not have the insight into his own problems and difficulties. However, in occasional instances, the neurotic may show good insight into his problems and defences. But he is still anxiety-ridden and unable to change. As such, there is a great deal of behaviour rigidity in the neurotic.

vi) **Disturbed interpersonal relations:** The neurotic is self-centred. He faces life with a heavy burden of helplessness and insecurity. He often feels he is fighting for his very life. The egocentricity and irritability of the neurotic hampers his satisfactory interpersonal relationships.

vii) **Unhappiness and dissatisfaction:** There are fears and conflicts because of which the neurotics are prone to be tense and pessimistic. The neurotic always feels that there is something wrong or something is missing in life. Therefore, he remains unhappy and dissatisfied.

viii) **Psychological and somatic symptoms:** Neurotics manifest a wide range of psychological and somatic symptoms. On the psychological level, these include anxiety, apprehension, phobias, obsessions and compulsions etc. Somatic symptoms include tension, fatigue, indigestion, excessive sweating, palpitations of heart, headaches, choking sensations and the like.

It may be pointed out that not all the characteristics of the neurotic are found in every case. Neuroses are the result of a complex interaction of personality and stress factors. The expressions of neurotic reactions are different for different individuals.

Classification of psychoneurosis

Let us now examine the various types of psychoneuroses on the basis of their symptomatology and aetiology. As early as in 1914, Freud had distinguished between neuroses caused by an existing nervous malfunction and the others caused by infantile painful experiences. Similarly, he differentiated between narcissistic and transference neuroses. The first ones are those in which the neurotic symptomatology is in a disguised form of an originally cathected object relationship. The second ones are those where the libido is turned towards one's own self. However, it is none of our aims to discuss psychoanalysis here, but these have been mentioned to provide some general information about Freud's classification of psychoneuroses. As such, we shall now discuss the classification of psychoneuroses, which has generally been accepted by psychologists.

(i) **Obsessive-compulsive neurosis:** Some writers have made an attempt to distinguish between obsessive neuroses and compulsive neuroses. As a matter of fact, obsessional neuroses cannot be separated from compulsion neuroses. Where obsessions predominate, compulsive behaviour is almost always present. Similarly, in compulsive neuroses, obsessional fears and doubts are also to be found.

By *obsessions* we mean persistent unwelcome ideas which, the patient realises are morbid but continue to bother him. These ideas are very close to paranoid delusions. A young teacher suddenly gets the idea that he is not the father of the six-year-old son he has always adored. This leads to the obsession that his wife is unfaithful.

By *compulsion* we mean persistent and irresistible desire or tendency to perform meaningless motor acts. The most frequent type of compulsion is the strong impulse to perform an act which appears senseless to others. The failure to perform such act causes anxiety. For example, the hand-washing mania.

We find compulsions with obsessions almost always. As a matter of fact, these protect the patient against obsession. The obsessional neurotic teacher, who doubts his wife's fidelity, becomes compelled to spy on her or even be compelled to lock his wife inside the house when he goes on duty.

(ii) **Anxiety neurosis, Neurasthenia:** It is the most common belief that all neuroses start with anxiety and many of the cases previously diagnosed as anxiety neuroses were only obsessional neuroses on one hand and anxiety hysteria on the other. Neurasthenia never occurs without some marked obsessional or hysterical content.

Obviously, the basic symptom of anxiety neurosis is anxiety of the free-floating type. Physical symptoms like respiratory troubles, vasomotor disturbances and perspiration are the most common. The patient does not know the cause of anxiety. Anxiety is a fear of harmless objects. In addition, there is usually irritability and insomnia, leading to an exaggerated feeling of fatigue, which reduces the capacity for work. The patient feels so depressed that he finds it difficult to perform his duties and social obligations.

An anxiety attack may be precipitated by some behaviour that is unacceptable to the ego; for example, masturbation and conscious guilt feelings, a sexual adventure, an episode of stealing or cheating or hostility expressed towards someone whose support the neurotic individual needs.

(iii) **Phobias:** By phobias we mean morbid fears of a situation or object. This may be allayed by not going in the vicinity of the situation or object except under certain special circumstances, like hydrophobia—an abnormal fear of water. Often quoted in the case of a young girl who went to a park in Paris with her mother and aunt when she was about seven years old. Late in the afternoon, the mother decided to return home but the child insisted on being permitted to stay for a while longer with her aunt. The mother agreed only when the child promised to observe strict discipline and would not go to the stream to play with water. It so happened that the aunt got busy talking with her friend and the child ran off alone to the river. While playing, she slipped and fell into the water. The child was scared because she had broken the promise she had made to her mother. The aunt assured her and promised, 'I will never tell.' The matter appeared to have ended there. However, when the little girl crossed the age of thirteen or fourteen years, she developed an extreme fear of water. At the age of twenty, she was treated with the help of psychoanalysis. When her aunt came visiting her again in Paris, the girl's mother received her at the railway station. On the way home, she learnt of the entire story of her illness from the girl's mother. When they reached home, the aunt saw the girl waiting for them at the gate. She kissed the girl and remarked, 'But I never told.' This connected the forgotten event of her life and she recovered completely.

Many phobias in adults are concerned with situations which normally cause fear in children, such as the fear of being closed-in or having no escape is called claustrophobia. The fear is a reaction formation against temptation because one has an even greater fear of the consequences of temptation. Besides, the phobias serve as protection against a situation, which might give rise to primary anxiety.

A phobia is often accompanied by dependence and helplessness. Thus, an individual with acrophobia—-fear of heights—may be willing to descend a long staircase only if accompanied by someone he trusts.

(iv) **Conversion hysteria:** During the nineteenth century, interest in conversion hysteria and hypnosis was combined with the realisation that the symptoms of conversion hysteria were due to self-induced hypnosis. The history of hysteria was, therefore, important because the study of this disease gave rise to the chief tenets of modern medical psychology. Hysteria refers to those symptoms of 'physical' disease which arise on a primarily psychological basis. The symptoms are always connected with the organs whose motor or sensory control is mediated by the central nervous system. They are distinguished from organ neuroses in that the organ neuroses affect organs innervated by the autonomic nervous system. They are distinguished from pathoneuroses as their origin is almost exclusively psychological. The psychologically determined hypo, hyper and para functions of the sense organs and musculature are often referred to as stigmata. In addition to the stigmata, there are episodic phenomena of hysterical nature, which range from hysterical 'epilepsies' to various mild nauseas and the like. Needless to say, in the concept of hysterical episodes are also included various dream states, somnambulism (walking in sleep), fugues (running away from home and forgetting the home address etc.) and personal amnesias (loss of memory, viz., forgetting the name of spouse etc.). Hysteria can be confused with nearly any physical disease.

The conversion patient also shows certain personality characteristics with fair degree of frequency, whereas organic patients have no particular personality pattern. Both male and female hysterics tend to be dependent, immature and suggestible. In some respects, they resemble the traditional 'spoilt child' with his overwhelming need for affection and fear of rejection. The personality of the potential or actual conversion patient is sometimes referred to as hysteroid. Rosenzweig and Sorensen (1942) conducted a study and have identified this personality pattern.

Relation with psychoses

Psychoneurotic mental illness is closely related to psychoses. Neuroses and psychoses diseases differ only in degree. In neuroses the mental illness is in mild form and in psychoses it is quite severe in nature. Neuroses can become psychoses if the patient is not properly looked after and given due care and proper therapeutic treatment.

There is some remarkable difference between neuroses and psychoses as the former class includes normal and mild types of mental diseases while the latter includes complex and grave types of mental disorders and diseases. The common thing is that both are, initially and primarily, related to mind and create difficulty in social adjustment of the affected individual. The difference between the two is more of quantity than quality. When psychoses are severe, reality is usually much distorted. Delusions and hallucinations represent attempts to deal with previously unconscious material, which invades preconscious and conscious organisations, as regression becomes widespread and ego boundaries begin to dissolve. Mild or borderline psychotic states may interfere little with normal life. They are sometimes chronic and are not recognised under ordinary conditions. Sometimes, neurotic disorders gain in complexity and it becomes difficult to treat them. This is when psychoneurotic disorders turn into psychotic defects.

Hysteria: symptoms, aetiology and treatment

One of the most important types of psychoneuroses is hysteria or hysterical neurosis. In hysteria, some parts of the body may stop functioning. These may be paralysis of limbs, deafness, blindness, cutaneous insensitivity or loss of memory, etc. The voluntary nervous system gets disordered or there is a clouding of consciousness. Normally, the symptoms appear suddenly. Similarly, the symptoms may disappear as suddenly as they appeared. There are two types of hysterical neurosis, viz., conversion hysteria type and dis-associative type. The term hysteria is derived from a Greek word, which means 'uterus'. Hippocrates thought this disorder took place in women only because of some sexual difficulties. He thought when sexual desires and desires for children were repressed strongly, it resulted in hysteria. Hippocrates thought marriage was the best remedy.

Conversion hysteria

This type is more common in women than in men. It is called conversion hysteria because the symptoms, that is, bodily disturbances, are merely conversions of repressed sexual urges. For example, if a person has a guilty feeling about masturbation, his hand might get paralysed. Of course, it is not a conscious process. The person, in fact, does not know why this has happened. He does not understand the meaning of this symptom. This is a Freudian explanation. Modern psychologists now believe that physical symptoms serve as a defensive function which enables the individual to overcome the stress. During war, hysterical symptoms are common among soldiers. They display paralysis of legs or inability to straighten their backs. This is a way of expressing unconscious wish to avoid going to the war front. Generally, this happens in extremely stressful situations. In cases of conversion hysteria, there is no organic basis.

General symptoms

There are various types of symptoms, classified under three heads – sensory, motor and visceral.

(1) **Sensory:** Any of the sensations like sight, touch, taste, smell or hearing may fail to function or these functions may get exaggerated or reduced or these may get distorted; or any combination or combinations of these may take place. For example, take the case of eyes. The person may not be able to see from one eye or both the eyes. His vision may get reduced. Or he may suffer from double-vision (diplopia). He may have tunnel vision when he can see only straight ahead and not on sides. Or, things may appear to him brighter than they actually are, or he may see things larger or smaller than their actual size. Things may appear blurred. There may be colour-blindness or jumbling up of printed letters while reading. He may suffer from pains all over the body, which he is unable to explain or locate. If the patient is distracted, the pain may be reduced, thereby showing that the pain is psychological rather than physiological.

(2) **Motor:** The person is not able to perform certain movements. There may be a sort of paralysis of fingers, limbs, voice etc. Tremors like shaking and trembling of limbs, fingers or head may take place. There may be twitching of muscles. The joints may become rigid. There may be walking disturbances.

Hysterical disturbance of speech may also occur. The person may be able to talk in whispers only. Or, he may become completely mute, when he cannot speak at all. Occasionally, there may be convulsions like those in epilepsy. However, there is a difference, the hysteric patient does not injure himself like an epileptic patient. The hysteric's pupillary reflex to light remains normal.

(3) **Visceral symptoms:** They are of many kinds—headaches, lump in the throat, choking sensation, respiratory difficulty, coughing spells, excessive appetite, persistent sneezing, loss of weight, recurrent fever and night sweats—all without any actual organic disease. The systems in conversion hysteria can be like any other disease. The diagnosis may become difficult. However, the following are some of the criteria to enable distinguishing a patient of conversion hysteria from a patient suffering from a similar organic trouble:

(i) There is little of anxiety and fear in a hysterical patient about his trouble. They are rather unconcerned about the long-range effects of their disease.

(ii) There is no wasting away. For example, a paralysed limb in the case of a hysterical patient will not atrophy even after a long time.

(iii) The dysfunctioning of the paralysed portions is only selective. For example, in hysterical blindness, the person does not bump into other people or objects. The paralysed muscles can be used for certain activities and not for others.

(iv) Under hypnosis, the hysterical symptoms can be removed.

Aetiology

The development of conversion hysteria usually follows the following pattern:

(i) The individual wishes to escape an unpleasant situation.

(ii) There is a suppressed wish to fall sick so as to avoid the situation.

(iii) Under continued stress, symptoms of some physical ailment appear. These symptoms depend upon a previous illness or those which the individual had witnessed elsewhere. If the patient already suffers from an ailment, then these symptoms are added to the ailment. A conversion pattern enables the individual to avoid or defend himself from a stressful situation. If the individual gets sympathy and support when he develops such symptoms, the reaction is reinforced. Such reaction pattern is maintained on subsequent occasions.

The conversion hysterics also show certain personality characteristics, which make them prone to conversion hysteria under stressful situations, which they wish to avoid. These characteristics are: over-dependence, immaturity and suggestibility. They resemble the 'spoilt child' with his strong need for affection and fear of rejection. Generally, such individuals have a history of over-protection and extra attention, when ill. They avoid all unpleasant aspects of reality. The precipitating cause of conversion hysteria is generally emotional stress and the need to escape from it.

Case study

The following is a case of conversion hysteria where the patient had a history of great emotional stress during her early childhood.

"The patient was a 27-year-old married woman who had suffered from headaches for eight years. She, then, began to suffer from nausea, vomiting, blurred vision and uncontrollable seizures. Of course, she did not lose consciousness or the ability to talk. She had never fallen, became blue, frothed at the mouth, bitten her tongue, otherwise injured herself, or lost control of her bowels or bladder, nor was there post-seizure amnesia. She was the eldest of four girls whose parents quarrelled continuously. Her father was an alcoholic. He molested her sexually when she was four years old. She contracted gonorrhoea. This led to her being removed from home by a welfare board for treatment and placed in a foster home with two elderly women and no children. She was frequently kept alone in a fenced yard and was not permitted to play with other children in the neighbourhood. Her social isolation lasted until she returned to live with her mother, at the age of six and began to attend school. Meanwhile, the father deserted the family. The mother repeatedly told the patient that she was just like her worthless father. The mother remarried when the patient was nine, but this marriage too was unsuccessful and ended in divorce. The patient did not get along with her stepfather.

She was no happier at school. She found the work difficult, was shy and introvert, and could never learn how to make friends. In the 10th grade, at the age of 16, she complained of abdominal pain (possibly of emotional origin) and her appendix was removed. She did not return to school but took up a series of brief-period jobs as a sales girl. She began to date a young man living next door, who was five years older than her. Her need for affection had been frustrated all her life and did everything to please him. She soon became pregnant. On being told, her mother responded, 'You made your bed, now lie in it.' The pregnancy led to a forced marriage. During the next eleven years, the patient had eight children. Her headache had begun when her second child was only five months old and, to her distress, she found she was pregnant again.

She and her husband were Catholics, but they used contraceptives occasionally. They felt guilty. She quarrelled with him without realising that the quarrels indicated their hostility to each other. Her unconscious hostility towards him led her to have an extramarital affair several years earlier. She believed that the affair led to one of her pregnancies. This, in turn, led to considerable guilt."

(Rosen, Fox & Gregory, 1972)

Treatments

Conversion symptoms can be removed by means of hypnosis. Also, psychotherapy can help such patients. An extensive treatment may be necessary, if the lifestyle is faulty. The faulty lifestyle may have to be replaced with the right one.

Dissociative hysteria: general symptoms

The major symptoms are amnesia, fugues, somnambulism and multiple personality. There is a good deal of disorganisation of personality resembling that of schizophrenia but, unlike schizophrenia, the symptoms start abruptly because of a stressful situation. However, these symptoms clear up soon.

Amnesia and fugue

Amnesia is a total or partial inability to recall past experiences. The forgotten material is there below the conscious level and can be brought to the surface under hypnosis. Generally, these experiences are traumatic in nature. The individual may not be able to remember his name, age, place of residence etc. He may not be able to recognise his parents, relatives or friends.

A fugue reaction is when the individual, in order to save himself from a stressful situation, actually runs away from it. He may wander away from home.

Somnambulism

It consists of walking, talking, eating etc. in a state of sleep. In such a state, the individual is neither awake nor aware of his actions.

Aetiology

In amnesia, the pattern is the same as in the case of conversion hysteria. In this case, the individual avoids thoughts of some unpleasant situation. In conversion hysteria, he avoids the unpleasant situation itself. In other words, it is conscious suppression of some traumatic event or situation. The personality that is likely to fall a prey to amnesia is generally egocentric, immature and highly suggestible. It is faced with an acutely unpleasant situation from which he sees no escape. The individual wishes to forget the situation and run away from it but does not accept it because it is too cowardly. When the situation becomes too intolerable, large parts of the personality and the situation itself are repressed. The case given below illustrates the motivational factors and sequence of events in a fugue.

Case study

A woman was found by the police in an empty parking lot. She was untidy in appearance and carried no purse or other possessions. She had no idea who, where or how old she was. Taken to the emergency department of a hospital, it was found that her feet were blistered and swollen, and she was dehydrated. However, no other physical or neurological difficulties were evident.

She was admitted to a psychiatric ward where she dressed neatly, ate and slept well, and socialised with other patients. During the interview she appeared somewhat anxious, unhappy, depressed and dependent. She complained of a lump in her throat and stated that she felt as though she was 'through a wet windshield'. However, she answered questions as best as she could, was soon correctly oriented for time and place. She was able to remember most of the events that had happened before the police found her. Prior to this event, she vaguely recalled having walked through the woods, but could not remember any other detail of her past life. She could form a mental picture of her mother but not of her father. She stated in anger, 'I don't want to know about him'. She had a pervasive feeling of personal loss but had no idea as to what she might have lost.

Three days after her admission to the psychiatric ward, she was subjected to hypnotism. She vividly recalled the details of her previous life. She was forty-three years old. She was the only child and had never known her father. Her mother had worked as a domestic servant in private homes and hotels. The patient had been able to live with her mother for only a few months at a time. The remainder of her childhood was spent with a childless middle-aged couple. Until the age of ten, she lived with the assumption that her father was dead. Later. she learnt from her mother that her father had deserted them before she was born. This information came as a shock to her. When she was fourteen, her mother committed suicide. The patient recalled having been so unhappy that she wished her mother had taken her too. She had made a number of friends in the few years previous to her mother's death, but she withdrew socially.

At eighteen, she married a factory worker but her marriage was unsuccessful from the beginning itself. Sexual relationships were unsatisfactory, the husband was unfaithful and drank excessively. Their finances were uncertain. After three children and several separations, the husband left her. The patient used to leave her children with her in-laws and go to work. She never got around to obtaining a divorce although she had led people to believe she had.

In her late thirties, she met a married man. She became deeply attached to him. His wife was a chronic patient in a mental hospital and he was unable to obtain a divorce. The patient lived with him as his wife, but she experienced an extreme sense of guilt. She wished they both were free to marry each other. She left him on two occasions to live with her in-laws, but she felt unwanted there. On the second such occasion she had an episode of amnesia and was found by the police while she was walking down a highway. The episode lasted only three days, after which she left to live with her male friend. Once again, the conflict proved too much for her and she left him to work in another city. While there, she received a communication from him that he had finally obtained a divorce and wished to marry her. She felt unable to tell him that she was not free to marry and was ambivalent about returning to live with him. She was trapped between her conflicts and her lie. She packed all her belongings in a suitcase, chucked it in a railroad station locker, put the key in a purse which contained all the money needed to buy a railroad ticket.

She lost the purse and also her memory. It was summer and, for the next several weeks, she slept outdoors and in abandoned houses. She was afraid of people and came out mainly after dark when she would walk aimlessly for hours. She was unable to recall eating or drinking. She was picked up by the police, on her forty-third birthday, close to a house where she had lived with her husband.

Treatment

The treatment is the same as for conversion hysteria. Hypnosis can clear up immediate amnesia. With the passage of time, amnesia may clear upon its own. When the stressful situation is removed, the cases of disassociative type of hysteria improve automatically. The patient can also be helped to learn more effective methods to face stressful situations so that attacks of disassociative hysteria do not reoccur.

Anxiety: symptoms, aetiology and treatment

Anxiety neurosis is the most common type of psychoneurosis. It is characterised by chronic anxiety. Of course, each individual has one anxiety or the other, but a normal person is able to live effectively with his anxieties. In the case of a normal person, the anxieties are genuine, he is always overcoming them through right actions. However, in the case of an anxiety neurotic, these anxieties are unreal and free-floating. Ross has defined anxiety reactions as 'a series of symptoms, which arise from faulty adaptations to the stress and strains of life…'

General symptoms

- An anxiety neurotic is tense and apprehensive.
- Experiences a vague, free-floating anxiety whose source is not known.
- Unable to concentrate.
- Difficulty in making decisions.
- Extremely sensitive.
- Easily gets discouraged.
- The trouble is generally accompanied by sleep disturbances.
- Perspiration levels are higher than others.
- The trouble may be accompanied by phobias, compulsions and other defensive reactions.
- He may be having chronic fear.
- Tolerance of frustration is low.
- He looks upon the world as basically threatening and cruel.
- Generally, he is diffident when it comes to handling a stressful situation.
- Those who are high in anxiety condition perform poorly on difficult tasks, particularly in the conditions of stress.

In an anxiety neurotic, normal anxiety and fear reactions are exaggerated. Many of the objects of fear are irrational and unjustified. The reaction, on the whole, is disproportionately strong to a minor threat. In the case of a normal person, the fear ends as soon as the danger is over. In an anxiety neurotic, the fear persists even after the danger is over. Actually, the neurotic has an unconscious fear, which is projected on to various objects in the environment.

The onset of anxiety neurosis may be sudden or gradual. It starts with anxiety attacks occurring off and on. In an anxiety attack, the person is terror-stricken and panicky. His automatic nervous system becomes overactive and he begins to perspire profusely. His heartbeat also increases. The person may feel dryness in the mouth and may begin to shudder and shake and he may become dizzy. He may feel an urgent need to urinate, suffer from diarrhoea, blurred vision and loss of appetite. He may have the feeling that his heart and head may burst. He may even feel that he is dying. He may become helpless and out of control. He may even actually wait for the anxiety neurosis attack to reoccur. After the attack, he is totally exhausted, emotionless and weak.

Aetiology

Anxiety neurosis shows that the person feels inadequate to face the inner and outer stresses perceived as threatening. Severe financial losses, loss of employment and other stresses may increase the otherwise general level of anxiety. The anxiety attacks are precipitated by a behaviour which is not acceptable to the ego. For example, guilt feelings after masturbation or a sexual incident, or an act of stealing or cheating, or hostility expressed towards someone whose support he needs.

Sometimes, the phantasies of undesirable behaviour make their way, breaking the individual's defences and cause severe anxiety although the undesirable phantasies are not translated into action. This heightened anxiety leads to new repressions; the individual is never aware of the significance of phantasies in the causation of his state of anxiety neurosis. Also, if the individual expects punishment or rejection by others, these may precipitate the anxiety attack. In many cases, the anxiety increases a good deal just before an examination or before a function where the individual is expected to make a good impression.

Anxiety becomes pathological when it becomes chronic and is provoked by ordinary stress situations, which a normal person is able to handle without much difficulty.

Anxiety reactions may be caused through 'conditioning'. A tense and anxious parent may transmit his anxiety to even an infant. If interactions with such a faulty model continue, the child may learn anxiety reactions through conditioning. It has been found that overanxious children tend to have neurotic mothers. If the parents have very high and unrealistic expectations from their children and they reject their actual accomplishments as substandard, they are paving the way for their children to become anxiety neurotics. Such children often adopt perfectionist parental standards and become critical of themselves if they fail to achieve that standard.

Case study

After ten years of a flourishing practice, a thirty-four years old dentist noted that his practice had declined slightly during the closing months of the year. Shortly after this, he began to experience mild anxiety attacks and complained of continual worry, difficulty in sleeping, and a vague dread that he was 'failing.' As a result, he increased his practice during the evenings from one to five nights. He began driving himself beyond all reason in a desperate effort to ensure the success of his practice. Although his dental practice now increased beyond what it had been previously, he still found himself haunted by vague fears and apprehensions of failure. These were augmented by frequent heart palpitations and pains, which he erroneously diagnosed as at least incapacitating, if not fatal, heart ailment. His anxiety became so great that he voluntarily sought assistance at a clinic.

Here was a case where the feelings of inadequacy and insecurity, and a slight threat of failure, led to an anxiety neurosis.

Anxiety neurosis also develops when an individual is unable to handle his dangerous impulses like aggression and hostility. The feelings are such that they must be controlled and denied at all costs to avoid possible rejection by others and to maintain an image of himself as a worthy person. Sometimes, he has phantasies of killing or injuring other people, even those who are loved and on whom the individual depends for acceptance and security.

Anxiety neurotic patients show unrealistic expectations and phantasies to harm. The degree of anxiety is related to the severity of anticipated harm. These expectations and phantasies are both physical and psychological dangers, such as being involved in an accident, becoming sick, being violently attacked, humiliation, failure and rejection.

The following case illustrates such an incidence of anxiety neurosis.

Case study

An eighteen-year-old male student developed severe anxiety attacks just before he went out on dates. Analysis revealed that he came from a very insecure home, in which he was very much attached to an anxious, frustrated and insecure mother. Intellectually capable and a good student, he had entered college at sixteen. But, during his two years at the campus, he had difficulty in getting dates with the college girls of his choice. For example, the student he had been dating recently would not make any arrangements to go out until after 6 pm of the same day, only after the chances for a more preferable date appeared remote. This increased his already strong feelings of inferiority and insecurity. This led to the development of intense hostility towards the opposite sex, mostly on an unconscious level.

About two months before coming to the college clinic for assistance, he had experienced the anxiety arousing phantasy of choking the young woman to death when they were alone together. As he put it, 'When we are alone in the car, I can't get my mind off her nice white throat and what would it be like to choke her to death.' At first, he put these thoughts out of his mind. However, the thoughts returned on subsequent nights with increasing persistency. To complicate the matter, he experienced his first acute anxiety attack. It occurred in his car on the way to pick up his date, but lasted only a few minutes. However, during the anxiety attack the young man was panic-stricken and thought he was going to die. After that, he experienced several more attacks under the same conditions.

The relationship of the repressed hostility to the persistent phantasies and anxiety attacks seemed clear in this case. Yet, it was not at all apparent to the young man, who was at a complete loss to explain either his phantasies or anxiety attacks. (Coleman, 1964).

Similarly, repressed sexual desires may threaten the individual to break through his defences and may cause great anxiety. This is so because repression is rarely complete and the individual is likely to have occasional attack of anxiety, although he may not know the reason of repressed sexual impulses.

Anxiety neurosis may also arise from indecision in cases of conflicts involving moral values or possible loss of security and status.

The following case illustrates the above.

Case study

A college girl named 'X' wanted to marry a young man she had met at school. However, he insisted on having premarital sex to ensure that they would be sexually compatible after marriage. This was contrary to her ethical and religious training. Although she was in love and found him physically attractive, she could not make up her mind. But the thought of giving in to his demands persisted. Eventually, she began to experience anxiety attacks, developed a serious difficulty in concentrating on her studies and suffered from insomnia. She would go over and over the conflict situation. When she came to the college clinic for assistance, it seemed apparent that two factors had contributed to the development of her anxiety attacks.

The first factor was a devalued self-concept; she viewed herself as unattractive, and was apprehensive about her relations with males. This basic insecurity and sense of inadequacy appeared to pave the way for the second factor, which precipitated the anxiety attacks, namely the conflict between her guilt-arousing desire for sexual relations she considered highly immoral and her fear of losing the man she loved if she continued to refuse. The situation was also fraught with other anxiety-arousing uncertainties. Even if she yielded to his demands, she had to face the possibility that he was only trying to seduce her, or even if he was sincere, he might not find her sexually compatible. In addition, she had vague feelings of apprehension that she would be somehow punished if she indulged in such behaviour. She might become pregnant, or he might lose respect for her.

Sometimes, when a stressful situation is like the one that earlier created trauma may produce intense anxiety in an individual who is basically insecure.

Case study

The following case is of an anxiety neurosis patient, whom the author treated successfully. He had strong feelings of guilt because of certain sex trespasses. His superego was very strong. At the same time, he found his sex urges uncontrollable. His ego could not balance the two – his superego and id impulses. His wife was not able to give him the sexual satisfaction he needed. The situation had resulted in strong repressions that triggered anxiety neurosis.

Treatment

Mild tranquilisers help anxiety neurotics for the time being but they do not effect a permanent cure. Psychotherapy is very effective. It makes them see their wrong style of life and enables them to see that some of their fears and dangers are imaginary. This also enables them to learn better and effective methods of coping with real difficult situations in life. The author has been successful in treating anxiety neurotics with 'Relationship Therapy' and 'Yoga Therapy'. These methods root out this illness permanently and develop a normal style of life in the individual, enabling him to face the hurdles in life with success.

Neurasthenia, Obsessive-Compulsive Neurosis, Phobia: symptoms, aetiology and treatment

Since all these illnesses belong to a common group-neurosis, there is much similarity in the aetiology, treatment and prognosis. Symptoms, however, differ clearly. Also, prognosis is poor in all these illnesses described here. These neuroses are much more disabling when compared to others.

Neurasthenia

Beard had first used the term Neurasthenia in 1863 and has the credit of popularising the term. According to the Diagnostic and Statistical Manual of Mental Disorders (DSM-II), neurasthenia is characterised by complaints of chronic weakness, easy fatigability and sometimes exhaustion. In the modern clinical practice, this diagnosis is rarely used and, therefore, as a separate diagnostic category not much is known. In the olden literature, it has been described to be an illness of women predominantly, and said to be confined mainly to those in the fourth and fifth decades of life. Mental and physical overwork, especially when it occurs in situations conducive to emotional tensions, have been labelled as precipitating factors. Other events also, such as the death of a loved one, excessive use of stimulants or narcotics, incurable fevers and abuse of sex are reported to produce these symptoms in individuals.

General symptoms

This disorder classically comprised complaints of mental and physical fatigue, associated with sensations of pressure in the head, poor memory, inability to concentrate, irritability of temper, poor sleep and various aches and pains. No major distortion of thinking and behaviour, no major hysterical symptoms of severe anxiety or bizarre compulsive acts are reported. The most characteristic symptoms of neurasthenia are listlessness and apathy that accompany the inner sense of exhaustion. The patient complains of fatigue, drops listless and lifeless into a chair or bed whenever he sits or lies down. He finds the symptoms unpleasant, distasteful and even painful.

Unlike a hysteria patient, he is awfully aware of his physical symptoms. He describes them in detail and is constantly seeking treatment.

Case study

The following case illustrates the incidence of neurasthenic disturbance.

A student, referred to the psychological clinic for failing work, complained of extreme lassitude, fatigability, vertigo and depression. He was unable to sleep at night and had no appetite. He stated he was allergic to all acid-containing foods. He had lost interest in his work and wanted to leave the college but his family objected. Examination of his past life revealed poor home adjustment. He was deeply attached to his mother but constantly quarrelled with his siblings and stepfather. For many years, he made it a practice of escaping difficulties by falling ill. During the previous four years, his personal medical bills totalled £1000/-.

Aetiology

Beard saw neurasthenia as being the result of an actual diminution of nervous energy. Janet, however, viewed all the neurotic illnesses, including neurasthenia, as the result of lowering of mental energy. Many authors gave importance to the hereditary constitutional factors as the predisposing cause. They attributed symptoms to either mental overwork or a prolonged discharge of emotions, which drained off the nervous energy to an excessive degree and lowered the total quantum below the critical level required for normal functioning. Freud too has followed the physical theoretical model proposed by others, but he also defined the mechanism that led to the symptoms. In his scheme, symptoms of neurasthenia were the result of excessive discharge of libido (sexual energy) through masturbations or nocturnal emissions (night discharge). As mentioned earlier, nowadays clinicians do not use this diagnostic category and lump these cases with other neuroses. Therefore, no systematic psychological or physiological observations are available.

Treatment

In the psychological form of treatment, individual insight or supportive psychotherapy, marital, family or group therapy or the need for environmental manipulations is indicated. Medication is frequently useful in such patients. However, if they are depressed or insomnia is noted, the short period acting barbiturates may be prescribed for bedtime.

Obsessive-Compulsive Neurosis

The term 'obsession' refers to the thought processes and the 'compulsion' to the related act. Aubrey Lewis defines it as a mental condition which is 'accompanied by a feeling of subjective compulsion' so that he does not willingly entertain it. On the contrary, he does his utmost to get rid of it. This definition contains three essential parts, viz., (1) There is a feeling of subjective compulsion. (2) The patient feels that it is baseless. (3) He tries to resist it. When he tries to resist, it provokes more anxiety and distress.

Obsession in one or other form is seen in most of the persons. Checking and rechecking the calculation, or checking the bolt of the door repeatedly at night, are some of the common obsessions. Symptoms of compulsion are most frequently found in children below ten years of age. Only a few of them start showing such symptoms in the fourth decade of life. It is generally found in the educated, well-to-do and upper strata of society. Gender-wise, there is no difference in its incidence. Nearly five percent of the neurotic patients are found suffering from this illness.

General symptoms

The simplest of the psychic symptoms are those in which thoughts, words or mental images are obtruded against the will into the conscious awareness of the patients. These thoughts are generally converted into actions. The patient performs certain actions regarding which he has awareness but is unable to control them. For example, the patient may say that he is fearful of catching the disease and, therefore, an idea comes to his mind that he should clean his body thoroughly. He takes bath several times a day. Some patients may have the idea that they should touch a particular thing for a fixed number of times, otherwise their near and dear ones may die. Some obsessive patients pray to get rid of bad thoughts. Some other may show that they may catch infections by touching a door or domestic articles; even the thought of having touched something infectious may create panic in them, forcing them to wash hands frequently.

These symptoms of obsessive-compulsive neurosis make the patient's life miserable. They appear nervous, depressed or worried. However, they are neatly dressed and well groomed. They are reserved and formal in their manners. Their movements are careful and precise without spontaneity. While giving the history of their illness, they provide every minor detail. They emphasise their sentences with such phrases as, 'in other words', 'to put it another way', 'for example', or 'to make it more clear'. They heavily rely on rational argument and talk in a highly intellectualised manner, no matter how simple the issue is. The attempt on the part of the examiner to hurry up is met with resistance from such patients. The work output of such patients declines to a considerable extent. They do not display hallucinations or delusions and their insight remains intact.

Case study

The following case illustrates a typical case of obsessive-compulsive disturbance.

'A successful businessman of fifty developed an overpowering fear of sudden death. This was especially marked at night when he had more time on his hands. The patient dreaded the thought of going to bed lest something terrible should happen during the night. He also exhibited many obsessions and compulsions. While undressing, he had to arrange his clothes in a definite manner. He felt that the number '3' was unlucky for him, so he carefully avoided touching objects three times by making it a point to touch them 18 times. His apprehensions about burglars and sounds in the house forced him to check and recheck the doors and windows many times during the night. The explanation and purpose of his ritualistic symptoms were brought out by psychiatric examination. The patient had been recently rejected for life insurance because of high blood pressure. This led to the fear that he might meet with sudden death. The elaborate ritual about clothes, burglars, and the number '3' served as distractions, keeping him fully occupied so that his thoughts would not dwell on his poor health and impending death.' (Condensed from Bagby, 1928).

Aetiology

The causes in obsession and compulsion are many and complex. The hereditary predisposition is aggravated by parental strictness and poor guidance. During their early childhood, they are given undue emphasis on neatness, cleanliness, duty, punctuality and perfectionism. In the personality structure, the obsessive-compulsive patients are introverted, sensitive, socially awkward, and with good intelligence—who compensate for their inability to make decisions and their feelings of insecurity by being extremely meticulous, over-conscientious and orderly.

Besides the above noted constitutional, heredity and early environmental factors, psychodynamic interpretations are also offered. The mental mechanisms involved in the development of such symptoms are repression, displacement and substitution. Repressed desires and memories are said to gain symbolic representation in the form of symptoms. In the Freudian terminology, there is—in obsessional neurosis—regression to the anal stage of libido, at which there has been a developmental fixation. During difficult situations, the individual regresses to this stage and shows the symptoms of this illness. The obsessive-compulsive symptoms are best interpreted as protective devices designed to absorb and neutralise the anxiety created by inner conflicts or opposition between desire and fear. For example, sexual temptation may be held in check by an obsessive fear of dirt or disease. An intense hatred for a person may be compensated for an intense fear lest he should kill him. This fear may lead to a compulsion to avoid touching knives. The repressed hostility is sometimes released by displacing it upon some neutral object. A simpler explanation is offered by substitution. The mind can be occupied with only one task at a time. If a person is kept constantly busy, counting steps, washing hands, repeating words etc., he has less opportunity to be troubled by more distressing thoughts. No doubt, the obvious symptoms are painful to the subject, but the knowledge of exact source of conflict would be still more painful to the ego.

Treatment

There are two main treatment procedures available for the treatment of any sort of mental disorder, viz., psychotherapy and physical treatment. The physical treatment is extremely limited in its scope and effect.

There is no specific drug for obsessive-compulsive neurosis. Tranquilisers and sedatives are often used, not so much to cure the illness as to reduce the associated depression, anxiety and sleeplessness. Occasionally, electric shock treatment is also administered but only to reduce depression. There have been a few reports where psychosurgery has been used.

Phobia

Phobia is a persistent fear of something which is not objectively a source of danger, but to which the patient reacts with real fear despite the fact that he realises his action is inappropriate. In this, all phobias are closely related to obsession. Phobias occur most frequently among young adults and are much more common among women than men. The following is the list of common phobias:

- Acrophobia – Fear of high places
- Agoraphobia – Fear of open places
- Claustrophobia – Fear of closed places
- Monophobia – Fear of being alone
- Nyctophobia – Fear of darkness
- Ochlophobia – Fear of clouds
- Zoophobia – Fear of animals

Many of us have some minor irrational fears. However, in phobic reactions such fears are intense and interfere with the phobic patient's daily routine. Such a person may painfully try to avoid the fear-arousing situations. The patient usually admits that he has no real cause to be afraid of a given object or situation, but is unable to help himself.

In addition to his phobia, the patient usually reports other symptoms like headache, back pain, abdomen upsets, feelings of inferiority, fear of having a serious illness etc.

Case study

An eighteen-year old girl had been given strict moral training concerning the evils of sex. Therefore, she associated sexual relations with vivid ideas of sin, guilt and hell. The basic orientation was reinforced when she was beaten and sexually attacked by a young man on her fifteenth birthday. Nevertheless, when the man she was dating kissed her and 'held her close' it aroused intense sexual desires which were extremely guilt-arousing. This resulted in a chain of avoidance behaviour. First, she stopped seeing him in an effort to get rid of her immoral thoughts, then she stopped all dating. She began to feel uncomfortable with any young man she knew. Finally, she became fearful of any social situation where men might be present. At this point, her life was largely dominated by her phobias. She became so 'completely miserable' that she requested professional help.

In the above case, the phobic reaction apparently served two protective functions, but these led to complications, too. As pointed out by Bagby and Shafter, phobias exhibit certain common features.

1. The phobic disturbance relates with a single traumatic episode, usually occurring in childhood.
2. The unpleasant experience is usually associated with some forbidden or shameful action.

3. The phobic reaction persists because related guilt or fear prevents the conscious recall of the original experience.
4. The phobic reaction may get generalised to a class of objects, similar to the original experience.

Aetiology

Hereditary, environmental and constitutional factors have been considered to some extent in the development of all the neurotic illnesses. However, the exact role of these factors is not very clear. Many psychologists feel that these factors are only predisposing. During stressful situations, they may show neurotic symptoms. Janet saw phobia as ultimately the result of the constitutionally based lowering of nervous energy, a concept that remained for him the starting point of all processes leading to neurotic illnesses. The abnormal discharge of the autonomic nervous system manifested as symptoms of anxiety. When these were combined with a pathologically heightened attention to bodily functions or to objects or situations in the external world, a phobic symptom was the result.

Freud has explained phobia on the basis of the mechanism of displacement. For him, anger, remorse, shame or anxiety not converted into a somatic symptom are displaced into some neutral or apparently insignificant idea, object or solution. Nowadays, phobia is understood on the basis of learning theories and is considered as a maladaptive behaviour.

Treatment

The treatment of this illness is similar to that of obsessive-compulsive neurosis. The treatment measures based on the model of learning theory are considered the best nowadays. There is, however, controversy about the outcome of the public illness. More or less, the points mentioned for the good prognosis of obsessive-compulsive are true for this illness also.

Author's Technique of Psychotherapy

I have been dealing with two categories of patients. In one category are those who call on me for a solution to a specific problem—be it emotional, social, intellectual or spiritual. Sometimes, one may have a number of problems in any of the said areas. In the other category are those patients whom I am required to visit at their homes. Often, I am approached through a relative of the patient because of the stigma attached to seeing a psychiatrist. The patient may be afraid of the psychotherapist or of people around. He is very aggressive. He is defiant and refuses to obey. The first step on my part in tackling such patients is always to establish rapport with them. Of course, it is easier to establish rapport with the first type than with the second. The reason is that the first type always approaches me with a certain amount of faith as he already has some knowledge of my technique.

In both cases, all efforts are made to make the patient feel at home. This is generally achieved by maintaining a very friendly attitude towards the patient. A cup of tea or a cigarette may sometimes help in achieving the purpose. A warm handshake, a word of praise or a friendly smile may go a long way in winning the patient's confidence. A calm demeanour, a pleasant atmosphere, a congenial environment may help in winning over the patient. Once the rapport is established, the treatment becomes an easy affair, provided the trouble is within the category of curable mental ailment.

The next step in my technique of psychotherapy may be called 'analysis', which is not the same as 'psychoanalysis'. The latter is a term applied to the method devised by Freud and thus associated with his name. the term 'analysis' is used here in a wider sense, and incorporates ideas from other disciplines as well. My technique is based on the assumption that certain personality disorders are of psychogenic origin. It includes a thorough study of the psyche of the subject—both the conscious and the unconscious make-up. Tools like free association, word association, colour association; projective techniques like free drawing; projective tests, viz., Rorschach, Thematic Apperception Test, Horn-Hellersberg Test, Sentence Completion Test, and a test devised by me called 'D' Test are employed to get a complete picture of the subject's psyche. The subject is provided with a permissive atmosphere to enable him to express himself freely—without any inhibition or restraint. For reaching the deeper levels of the psyche, hypnoanalysis may also be employed. Under hypnotic state, effort is made to get at the forgotten experiences of the subject. Tape-recording, stenography and note-taking are used for recording the material thus obtained.

The data is subjected to analysis so as to get at the personality syndrome of the individual. The defective and faulty personality patterns are located and taken note of. Complexes, conflicts and deep repressions are identified. Before particular complexes are taken to have been completely diagnosed, they are validated by different means. The entire approach is elective. The idea is a systematic and persistent exploration of a neurotic patient's mental process in order to help him towards better personal and social integration.

The next step in my psychotherapy may be called 'psychosynthesis'. The subject is helped to psychosynthesise his personality pattern afresh so as to eliminate the faulty make-up. He is helped to resolve his complexes and conflicts. He is provided an opportunity to give vent to his repressions. He is helped to build up a healthy personality pattern. Different techniques like suggestion and persuasion are used for the purpose. Models for imitation are presented. Prestige suggestion, wherever desirable, is made use of. The subject is trained in the techniques of auto-suggestion. Books and other literature are provided to the subject according to his level. As soon as the subject is normal and develops sufficient confidence to fight his own battle of life, transference is effected. He is gradually weaned away to make him stand on his own feat. Whereas 'analysis' is the separation of the whole into component parts in order to understand the personality make-up, 'psychosynthesis' is integration of all the functions and of all the potentialities and drives of the individual. In other words, it is placing together or combining together of parts into an integrated whole. This enables a human being to give harmonious expression of the totality of his nature—physical, emotional, mental and spiritual. In psychosynthesis, the various tendencies of human nature are harmonised. This synthesis is effected around the centre. To start with, this synthesis takes place around the conscious ego and, later, it may take place around a deeper 'self', which some have designated as 'spiritual self'. This 'spiritual self' may be understood as universal human values like truth, honesty, love, service, humility etc. This synthesis around the spiritual self enables one to realise his oneness with the cosmos. There is, what we call, 'spiritual drive' in man. The repression of this drive can lead to neurosis in just the same way as the repression of sexual and aggressive drives do. Psychosynthesis enables the individual to get to know this 'spiritual' drive and utilise it for the reconstruction of the personality. Yogic exercises, if necessary, are recommended for concentration and meditation.

Assagioli, in his article, *Dynamic Psychology and Psychosynthesis*, has distinguished various stages of psychosynthesis. They are as follows:

Knowledge of one's personality: This may be compared to our analytical stage, where the individual gets a view of his personality make-up through free association, word association, colour association and projective techniques etc.

Dis-identifying ourselves: This involves dis-identifying from the non-Self and identifying with the Self, for example, to be aware I have a body but I am not my body. I have a body I use just as I use my bicycle. Here, the individual realises that his 'self' is separate from his body and emotions etc.

Realisation of one's true self: Here the true self, that is the unifying centre, is discovered.

Psychosynthesise itself: Here, the person reconstructs a personality around his true self, i.e., the higher values of life—truth, love, service and humility etc.

Methods

Two methods have been employed in the psycho-therapeutic work reported in this volume—first, the case history and, second, the clinical observations. The shortcomings of one method have been complemented by the other. The material collected by both these methods is organised for evaluation. For the case history, the interview technique has been employed.

Interview

This is the method most frequently used in cases reported here. Interviews ranging from one to even more than one hundred have been held with the subjects depending on the nature and extent of the maladjustment. Observations of external appearances, gestures, movements, modes of speech, behaviour under different situations and questionings have been recorded. Data has been collected even with the help of self-recording techniques. The association material—both from free and constrained—and dreams material have been collected.

Psychological tests

The following tests were employed depending upon the type of the subject.

- The Association Tests

- The Rorschach Test
- The Thematic Apperception Test
- The Children Apperception Test
- Sentence Completion Test
- The Drawing Completion Test

The Association Tests

(a) **Word Association Test:** This test is designed to study the associative content and process of the subject. The list of words used is more or less the same as given by Rapaport in his book, *Diagnostic Psychological Testing*, and was prepared by Dr William D. Orbison. The words are: 1) World. 2) Love. 3) Father. 4) Hat. 5) Breast. 6) Curtains. 7) Trunk. 8) Drink. 9) Party. 10) Bowel movement. 11) Book. 12) Lamp. 13) Rug. 14) Chair. 15) Boyfriend. 16) Penis. 17) Dark. 18) Depressed. 19) Spring. 20) Bowel. 21) Suicide. 22) Mountain. 23) House. 24) Paper. 25) Homosexual. 26) Radiator. 27) Girlfriend. 28) Screen. 29) Masturbate. 30) Frame. 31) Man. 32) Orgasm. 33) Movies. 34) Cut. 35) Laugh. 36) Bite. 37) Woman. 38) Dance. 39) Dog. 40) Daughter. 41) Taxi. 42) Mother. 43) Table. 44) Beef. 45) Nipple. 46) Race. 47) Water. 48) Suck. 49) Horse. 50) Fire. 51) Vagina. 52) Farm. 53) Social. 54) Son. 55) Taxes. 56) Tobacco. 57) City. 58) Intercourse. 59) Hospital. 60) Doctor. This set includes words pertaining to family, home, oral and aggressive and sexual type. So, this list is able to explore various types of conflicts that are prominent in different types of maladjustments. The test consists of two parts. In the first part, the subject is asked to give as quickly as possible the first word that comes to his mind after hearing each stimulus-word. In the second part, the stimulus words are read to the subject again, and he is asked to reproduce his original response to each stimulus word. The word association list contains words that touch upon specific conflicts; for example, mother 'hate it', girls 'dangerous'. The responses to these words show the two areas of conflict. However, if there is no response to a stimulus word or it is unusually delayed, it is indicative of the fact that the conflict in that area is present but the exact nature of the conflict cannot be known unless we probe further. The response merely indicates that those stimulus-words for which no or delayed or particular types of reactions are found, were connected with complexes charged with emotions.

(b) **Word Colour Association Test:** It is just like the (a) above, except that here the subject is required to name a colour in response to the word spoken. The list of words is given below.

Word Colour Association List

1. Mountain
2. Water
3. Cart
4. House

5. Earth
6. Gambler
7. Peace
8. Cow
9. Jealousy
10. City
11. Weapon
12. Child
13. Sleep
14. Attack, Quarrel
15. Father
16. Cow-dung
17. Pain
18. Official
19. Field
20. Taboo, Untouchability
21. Orphan, Poor
22. Shame, Blush, Shy
23. Intoxication, Drunkenness
24. Sister
25. Village
26. Happy
27. Parda
28. Death
29. Gossip
30. Grandfather
31. Labour
32. Vagina
33. Opium

34. Concentration
35. Love
36. Study
37. Anger
38. Hunger
39. Teacher
40. Insane
41. Boy, Son
42. Liar
43. Daughter
44. Sadhu
45. Wedding
46. Maternal uncle
47. Monsoon
48. Mother
49. Faeces
50. Clown, Joke
51. Penis
52. Trance
53. Religious gathering
54. Family
55. Pot
56. Money
57. Birds
58. Land
59. World
60. Bed
61. Stealing
62. Water buffalo

63. Power
64. Bullock
65. Mother-in-law
66. Crop
67. Father-in-law
68. Escape
69. God
70. Daughter-in-law
71. Devote
72. Caste
73. Effeminate/Homosexual
74. Trouble
75. Brother
76. Semen
77. Guest
78. Buttock
79. Wife or Husband
80. Law
81. Sexual intercourse
82. Laughter

The Rorschach Test

This is the most popular projective technique that has been used with great success for the testing of personality and maladjustment. It is an important tool in the hands of psychotherapists for clinical diagnosis. A good deal of work has been done in developing it into a scientific and clinical tool. More than one thousand books and articles have been published on it. There is a special journal called the *Journal of Projective Techniques* that is devoted to the publication of research on this test. Rorschach, the Swiss psychiatrist, prepared this test. He administered a large number of inkblots to his mental patients and selected ten, which he published together with his monograph, *Psychodiagnostik*. Some of the ten blots are black-grey white and some are coloured. They are presented in turns before the subject. The subject is asked what he sees in each or what it makes him think of. The responses of the subject are jotted down. After the administration, the responses are discussed with the subject just to find out what determined them and their location. Klopfer and Kelley advocated the third stage also, called 'Testing the limits'. At this stage, the tester tries to probe deeper and prompts the subject to give more responses if he can.

Scoring: For scoring, the total number of responses in each case is taken into consideration. Each response is studied with respect to three aspects, viz., location, determinant and content. Location means the area to which the response belongs. It may be a whole blot (W) when the subject uses the whole inkblot to give one response. He might say in response to the first card that it is a 'bat'. He may base his response on a large portion of the blot (D) as in the case of second blot, he says, 'Two clowns are fighting'. He may base his response in some small usual detail (d).

Determinant: By determinant is meant the characteristic of the blot that helped in the determination of the blot. The determinants are the shape or form of the blot (F), colour (C), movement (M) and shading (K). It also indicates whether the form of response fits well (F+) or poorly (F-). The response may also depend upon the shape and colour (FC) of the blot, or shape and shading (FK) of the blot. The responses are further analysed as human beings, parts of animals, nature and inanimate objects. Each response is further classified as a response occurring very frequently (P) or as an original response (O). A chart showing frequency of each category and numbers of ratios between different categories are worked out. On the basis of these, interpretations are done.

Interpretation: Interpretation of Rorschach responses can only be done by persons having a good psychological background and a good deal of working with the Rorschach cards. The method of interpretation as given by Klopfer and Kelley is given below.

Number of Responses (R) and Rejection of Cards

1. **Significance of the total number of responses:** The range of responses in the case of adults is between 20 and 40. Children below 10 years, subjects with severe lesions of the central nervous system, severely blocked subjects and subjects with subnormal intelligence have an average of less than 20 responses. A good number of high form level are indicative of intellectual level. If the number of such responses is less than 9 in the case of an adult, it becomes doubtful whether the person is normal. If the number of such responses of the high form level

is more than 75, it is an indication of the fact that the subject is brilliant.

2. **Significance of rejections:** Rejection of cards II, IV, VI and IX is less significant than the rejection of any of the other cards. If such a subject persists in rejection of the cards even during the inquiry and in testing-the-limits, the chances are that he may be a psychotic. Neurotic subjects in the majority of cases are able to overcome their blocking either spontaneously during the inquiry or by a special request during the testing-in-limits. If the rejection of the card is because of intellectual capacity, added pressure in testing-the-limits at the most produces inaccurate or nonsensical responses. Neurotic subjects generally reject cards II, IV, VI and IX or VIII and X, because of the colour situation or because of the shading. If more than four cards are rejected—especially not the normal ones but the ones which are usually accepted—for no reason, it is a pointer towards psychotic disorder.

Time factor

1. **Average time per response (Response Time):** The average is between 30 seconds and 60 seconds. An average time per response of more than 90 seconds is found only among subjects with some rather severe pathology or extreme inhibitions.

2. **Average time before first response to each card (Reaction Time):** If the average reaction time

to the achromatic cards and to the coloured card is more than 10 seconds, it has an interpretative significance.

Relationship among content categories

1. **Percentage of Animal Responses (A%):** A great number of A and Ad responses indicates narrow range of interests of the subject. Responses, besides those of human and animal, are indicative of diversity of interest.

2. **Popular and Original Responses:** If the subject does not use the most obvious concept used by the majority of other subjects, it may mean that the subject is not willing to do so. The use of 5 or more popular concepts shows that the subject possesses the capacity and interest in thinking along the same lines as other people. In the case of a superior subject, the number of original responses (O) reaches or exceeds popular responses (R) but there is a minimum of 5 in either case. Again, the quality of the original responses is quite high.

Whole figures and part of figures (H+A): (Hd + Ad)

Most of the subjects see a more or less complete human or animal figure rather than only a part of such a figure. If a subject sees only profiles, heads, legs and hands or any other parts of human or animal body, the possibility is that the subject has a tendency to be more critical. It has been roughly determined that threshold for such a critical attitude is reached if the number of Hd + Ad exceeds the number of H+A.

The Thematic Apperception Test

Another projective test called Thematic Apperception Test is usually referred to as TAT. It was originally devised by Murray and Morgan in 1935. It consists of a series of pictures about which the subject tells stories. The test is based upon the fact that when a person interprets an ambiguous social situation, he is likely to reveal his own personality. The test has been so named because it reveals basic 'themes' that recur in the imaginative productions of a person. Apperception means a readiness to perceive in certain ways on the basis of one's personal experiences. So, as the name signifies in the test, the subject interprets an ambiguous stimulus according to his individual readiness to perceive in certain ways.

The subject's main task is to frame a story on the picture. The examiner says, 'I am going to show you some pictures. I want you to tell me a story about what is going on in each picture. What led up to it and what will the outcome be?'

The story told by the subject recorded verbatim.

Scoring and Interpretation

Many schemes have been worked out for scoring TAT material. The interpretation and the test depend upon the purpose for which the test is administered. Each story is analysed. Each need and press receives a weight score. The needs and presses are then arranged according to their ranks. At the same time, the relationship between the needs are investigated. The present method of scoring studies comprises the style of the story, i.e., the length of the story, language used, originality, variation of content and organisational qualities. The themes that recur in the stories are taken note of. The relation of the outcome of the story with the rest of the plot is studied. The primary and secondary identifications are determined. The main clues for the interpretation are the recurring themes.

Procedure

The subject is seated in a comfortable chair with his back to the examiner and the following directions are read out to him:

This is a test of your creative imagination. I shall show you a picture. I want you to make up a plot or a story for which it might be used as an illustration. What are the relationships among the individuals in the picture? What has happened to them? What are their present thoughts and feelings? What will be the outcome? Do your best. Since I am asking you to indulge in your literary imagination, you may make your story as long and detailed as you wish.

Test material

The material consists of 19 pictures printed on white Bristol board and one blank card—making a total of 20 pictures. There are two sets of pictures. Each set is divided into two series of ten pictures each. About an hour is devoted to a series. The two sessions are separated by a day or more. If necessary, test administration is followed by an interview.

Children's Apperception Test C.A.T.)
History

The idea of CAT was conceived by Ernst Kris. He thought children could identify themselves with animal figures more readily than with persons. It was felt that TAT was meant for adults and so could not meet the children's needs. Similarly, the Picture Story Test could not be used prior to adolescence. The CAT was prepared for children aged between 3 years and 10 years. Violet Lamout drew the pictures according to the suggestions of the authors. She drew 19 pictures. Sets of these pictures were distributed to some child psychologists for trial. On the basis of his experience, ten most useful pictures were selected.

Nature and purpose of the Test

The test consists of ten pictures depicting animals in various situations. The CAT is a projective method, i.e., 'a method of investigating personality by studying dynamic meaningfulness of the individual differences in perception and standard stimuli.' CAT is good for children of the age-group of 3 to 10 years. Symonds-Picture-Story test is good for adolescents and adults. The CAT pictures are designed to elicit responses generally, to investigate problems of sibling rivalry, to illuminate the attitudes towards parental care, to learn about the child's relationship to the parents as a couple—technically spoken of as the oedipal complex and its culmination in the primal scene, namely, the child's fantasies about seeing the parents in bed together. Related to this, we wish to elicit the child's fantasies about aggression, about acceptance by the adult world, and his fear of being lonely at night with a possible relation to masturbation, toilet behaviour and the parents' response to it. We wish to learn about the child's structure and his dynamic method of reaching to and handling his problems of growth.

Administration

First, a good rapport must be established. Whenever possible, CAT should be presented as a game. The child may be told that we are going to play a game in which he is to tell a story about pictures, that he should tell what is going on, and what the animals are doing now. At suitable points, the child may be asked what went on in the story before and what will happen later.

Interpretation

In interpreting the stories, it is to be seen what the child makes of the pictures, and why. Rather than judging by one story, it is safer if we find a common denominator or trend in a number of stories—what may be called the theme of the story.

It is to be seen, with what figures the subject mainly identifies himself as the hero, the hero being the figure around whom the story is primarily woven. There may be more than one hero. Probably, the interests, wishes, deficiencies, gifts and abilities with which the hero is invested are those which the subject possesses, wants to possess, or fears that he might have. It is important to know as to what self-image the subject has, the way the child sees the figures and how he reacts to them. Again, it is important to know with whom in the family the child identifies. The figures introduced in the story but not shown in the picture should be taken note of. If some figures in the picture are omitted or ignored in the story so related, its meaning may be an expression of the wish that the figure or object were not there. This may mean plain hostility. Main anxieties of the child should be determined. The most important anxieties are physical harm, punishment, fear of losing love and of being deserted. Again, it will be useful to note the defences that the child takes, e.g., flights, passivity, aggression, orality, acquisitiveness, renunciation, regression etc. Main conflicts and their nature should be studied. The relationship between crime committed in the story and severity of the punishment meted out for it gives us a good measure of the child's superego development. It should be noted whether the story ends happily or not. From this we know whether the child is depressed and hopeless, or cheerful and optimistic. From the stories, the maturation level of the child can also be studied. We may try to know whether the child is functioning above, below or consistently with what one could expect at that chronological age. The intellectual level can be studied from the language used, conceptualisation and structure of the stories.

Sentence completion Test (S.C.T.)

The sentence completion test is a variation of the Word Association Method. The SCT decreases the number of associations by making the stimulus directive rather than non-directive. It is better able to suggest contexts, tones of feelings, qualities and specific objects or areas of attention. It allows greater individual freedom and variability of response, and it takes a larger area of the subject's life. The method was first used by Ebbinghaus in 1897 to test intelligence. Tendler used this method as a test for various emotions. Lorge and Thorndike tried to determine the personality traits with the help of this method and evaluated the responses statistically. Rhode used the SCT for clinical work to determine the needs, inner conflicts, fantasies, sentiments, attitudes, aspirations and adjustments of the clients. Rhodes-Hindreth Completions Blank consists of 64 items. It is intended for individuals who are approximately 12 years of age. The author claims that her test determines the subject's needs, inner states, traits, press, tastes, sentiments, ideology, ego structure, intellectual status and emotional maturity. On similar lines, Shore constructed Self-Idea-Completion Test (S.I.C.), the difference being that in SIC, the incomplete parts suggest contexts, feeling tones, qualities of attitude and specific objects or areas of attention. From psychological point of view, Shore's test is important.

Stein devised a Sentence Completion Test as an aid in the selection of officers of strategic services personnel during the war. It attempted to elicit information on such points as family, past drives, inner states, goals, cathexes, energy, time perspective, reaction to others and reaction of others to the subject. Symonds used this type of test in the Strategic Services Assessment Programme. It studied persistence, striving for success, feelings of inferiority, doubt and worry, depression and discouragement following failure, high standards, and emotional stability in stressful situations. Rotter and Willerman used this very method as an evaluative technique and claimed a fairly high validity for this technique. Their Incomplete Sentence Test (I.S.T.) was used as a screening device in Army/Air Force convalescent hospitals. Joseph M. Sacks and other psychologists of the New York Veterans Administration Mental Hygiene Service designed a sentence completion test to obtain significant clinical material regarding the family, sex, ideas of interpersonal relationship of the family members and others. It also focused on the self-concept of each patient. The author devised a Sentence Completion Test consisting of 99 incomplete sentences to study how far the B.T. students of the Government Training College, Jalandhar, were adjusted to their environments.

The subject was required to complete these sentences as quickly as possible. The sentences selected were such as touched upon nearly every aspect of a student's life in the Government Training College, Jalandhar. They attempt to explore significant areas of the students' adjustment. For example, there are sentences designed to elicit interpersonal relationships of the subject, their family members, friends and relatives. They attempt to determine their attitudes towards college hostel or residence, opposite sex and teaching profession. They try to find out their main drives, worries, annoyances, fears and troubles. They endeavour to tap information about their health, economic condition, studies etc.

The Drawing Completion Test
Horn-Hellersberg Test

The test was originally devised by Carl Horn, an Art teacher of the Rochester Athensean and Mechanics Institute, Rochester, New York. He took the various lines in the blanks from famous paintings. Dr Elisabeth Hellersberg standardised it as a personality test, used for testing the 'Individual's Relation to Reality' and as an instrument for social, cultural and individual diagnosis. The author standardised the test for measuring Imagination and Emotional Maturity of the Postgraduate Teacher Trainees.

The author also studied the H.H. responses of the abnormal adults and their behaviour.

Results

1. There is more of Ego-projection in mental patients than in normal subjects. By projection here, we presume that there is always some element of the unpleasant, the unwanted and the morally undesirable about the projected trait. Out of a total of 19 mental patients, 5 showed projection in their responses. In the case of normal adults, of the 148

subjects only 4 showed some projection. Some of the projected material as given by the mental patients is: (a) 'P' in the course of the interview that follows the test, says about rectangle (O) – I have drawn one doctor and one patient. The patient is dead tired of his or her life. He has done everything that he could. Now he has lost all his hope, but when he gets terrible attack from the disease, he wants some way to get out of it. Again, he goes and tells the people he meets if they could suggest something. Then this patient goes into a wood that he would be cured but the result is the same as before, so his energy is exhausted now and he is puzzled with his own problems. Then, she goes on to say, 'I did this because I am the person who is the patient, who is always in search of doctors. So, some people really sympathise with me and some say it is 'elergic', and some call it psychological. I interpreted my own self in the picture.' (b) 'J', a mental patient, draws something in rectangle 'L' and writes underneath it, 'Lap of women', and, during the course of the interview, he reveals that he has drawn this because he greatly desired to sit in the lap of a woman. Then he feels a sense of guilt and says that the thoughts of sex worried him.

2. The number of the 'Whole' responses is less in the case of psychopaths than in the case of normal persons. The percentage of 'Whole' responses

among normal persons is about 95%, whereas in the case of mentally disturbed patients, it is only 30%.

3. There is preponderance of simple, discrete, uncoordinated sketches having no relation—verbal or spatial—in the case of mentally disturbed patients. Out of the 19 patients studied, only 5 could draw meaningful sketches, the rest drew uncoordinated sketches.

4. Schizophrenic types of patients drew mostly lifeless figures.

5. Among mentally disturbed patients, the frequency of sharp-edged weapons like swords, knives, spears, guns and pistols etc. was about 30% as compared to 8% among normal subjects. May be such a great predominance of these drawings is indicative of a state of great mental tension of the mentally disturbed patients. Anyway, the responses point out to a very significant feature of the subject with a dangerously aggressive tendency.

6. One of the mentally disturbed patients showed extreme projection. He seemed to be greatly obsessed with the idea of sex. In practically all the diagrams, he drew sexual parts and all the time he was associating with them. For example, in rectangle B, he draws a vagina and says the drawing is connected with his mother and sister. He says that it is perversion but cannot help it and so wants to commit suicide. In rectangle N, he draws 'A cobra with its mouth wide open' and says it is associated

with his castration fear, which is one of his greatest fears. In rectangle A, he draws a 'worm' and says it represents penis. The penis goes into the vagina like a worm. Then he curses himself and says how wicked he is.

7. A few mentally disturbed patients showed morbid and horror images, which were not clear. For example, in rectangle H, one of the mentally disturbed patients draws 'a witch', and says he is afraid of it.

8. The drawings of this patient are marked by a lack of preciseness and uniformity. For example, in human figures, the parts of the body shown are quite disproportionate. Either the head is drawn too large or the legs are too short. In some cases, essential parts of the body like ears, nose, eyebrows, etc. are missing.

9. The manner of approach of mentally disturbed patients is mostly impulsive and they show diffidence. For example, they would suddenly scribble out something meaningless, continue scribbling for a while, and then may stop altogether and say, 'I don't know what to make'. Sometimes, it becomes very difficult for the examiner to enable him to overcome the diffidence.

10. The mentally disturbed patients are generally distracted and are restless during the test and they give up the task very often. They may work for a few minutes but then may start looking hither and thither.

Their looks may betray a sort of vacantness about them. They may start making unnecessary movements, viz., rocking in the chair, moving legs to-and-fro, tapping the floor with feet etc.

11. While taking the test, some patients show a good deal of emotional excitement and make unnecessary and meaningless gestures.

With the help of various techniques mentioned above, the case history of the patient is prepared in as great a detail as possible for diagnostic purposes. The case history contains the following information:

Identification data, problems of the patient, his life—including information obtained from the patient, relatives and acquaintances; the referring physicians consulted previously by the patient. This information comprises familial, developmental, educational, vocational and medical history, history of the present illness, data of physical examinations regarding the perceptual, intellectual, emotional aspects etc., the psychological testing reports, interviews with the psychoanalyst, patient's life in the hospital, patient's sexual life, case analysis, giving how the present maladjustment of the patient had been brought about, a case summary containing psychiatric picture, the symptomatic and the social diagnoses, treatment recommendations and the statement of prognosis.

Psychosynthesis

For the full integration of personality, psychosynthesis is a necessity. Psychosynthesis has been very well explained by R.K. Assangioli.

Psychosynthesis of R.K. Assangioli and Yoga of Sri Aurobindo

What Aurobindo calls 'Psychic Being' Assangioli designates as 'True Self'. Each gives a method of integrating the various sub-personalities of the individual. The initial stage is body-mind integration. Both body and mind interact upon each other. This synthesis is followed by body-mind-spirit integration. This trio leads to complete synthesis and is designated as 'Psychosynthesis' or complete integration of personality. Achieving this complete synthesis is a lifetime process. For the body-mind integration, we have to deal with sub-personalities like physical, emotional and mental. Any defect in the development of these sub-personalities results in an obstacle to complete synthesis or full integration. If there are any defects, they ought to be removed first by psychoanalysis, psychotherapy, cognitive therapy, relationship therapy or yoga, or any combination of these, and other techniques.

Next comes the subconscious of the mental make-up of the personality, from where the various conflicts, complexes, prejudices and repressions etc. have to be removed because it is them that cause various psychological troubles. This is achieved through various techniques like projective tests, dream analysis, word association test and self-analysis through meditation etc. After this, the individual is ready for the psychosynthesis which enables him to raise his consciousness level. The raising of consciousness level leads to the resolution of various problems; the lowering of consciousness leads to all sorts of psychological abnormalities. The raising of consciousness is achieved through meditation of many kinds. One can choose any one type of meditation according to his personality make-up and stick to it until the object is achieved.

According to Anthony Campbell, there are seven states of consciousness:

1-3. Dreamless, Dreaming and Waking States of Consciousness: When there is no awareness of the self. Here, the self means the real Self and not the small self that pertains to body only.

4. Transcendental Consciousness: Here, the awareness of the self is present.

5. Cosmic Consciousness: Awareness of the self is present and it leads to perception.

6. God Consciousness: Awareness of the self is present and awareness of the outer world is also present.

7. Unity Consciousness: In this state, not only the awareness of the Self and the world is present but also conflicts are resolved. Anthony Campbell has taken this idea from Maharishi Mahesh Yogi's book, *The Science of Being and Art of Living*.

These states of consciousness can be achieved by various methods. In Indian psychology, the method employed is yoga and meditation. As far as yoga is concerned, there are many books available. Some of the most important being *Light on Yoga* by B.K.S. Iyengar, *A Gem for Women* by Geeta S. Iyengar, *Solar Yoga* by Yogacharya Jankiraman and Carolina Rosso Cicogna, *Asana, Pranayam, Mudra, Bandas* by Swami Satyanand Saraswati, *Yoga Therapy* by Dr R.K. Garde, *Psychotherapy in India* by Dr H.G. Singh, *Yoga Technique of Psychotherapy* by Dr H.L. Sharma, *Western Psychotherapies and Hindu Sadhana* by Hans Jacobs, and *Pranayam* by Swami Kuvalyananda etc.

Regarding meditation, there are many techniques devised by various yogis. Some of the important techniques are:

1. TM technique by Maharishi Mahesh Yogi.
2. Vipeshyana Technique by Sri S.N. Goenka.
3. Brahm Kumari's and Brahm Kumar's technique.
4. Satya Sai Baba's technique.
5. Beas Dera's technique.
6. Zen technique of Buddhists.
7. Diabetical technique by Haridas Chaudhari.
8. Bhajan Yoga's technique.
9. Sufi's technique.
10. Gurdjieff's Technique.
11. The Africa Training.

12.Ramakrishna technique

13.Sri Paramhans Yoganand technique.

I have been using a very simple technique for my patients, such as:

1. We start with a few 'hath yoga' exercises, and pranayama to relax the body and mind. The yoga exercises chosen are according to the age, stage of development and sex of the patient. His physical and mental health are always taken into consideration before prescribing these exercises.

2. The patient is helped to concentrate from concrete objects to abstract ideas.

3. Meditation on the personal God (Isht Deva) with and without the help of his/her picture or image.

4. Meditation on real 'Self'.

5. Meditation on 'Self' merging into 'Cosmic Self'.

6. Meditation on being merged into the Cosmos etc.

There are many misconceptions about meditation, created knowingly or unknowingly by the teacher of meditation. The most widespread misconception is that meditation is possible only by reciting a particular mantra contained in a particular religious book. This is totally wrong. The main idea in meditation is concentrating on an object bestowed with certain good qualities or an idea or ideas which are good for the individual or a person whom the individual admires and whose qualities he himself wishes to acquire. By meditating on these qualities, he himself begins to imbibe those good qualities and thus raises the level of his consciousness, which leads to vertical development of his personality. The result of the meditation is that the person gradually becomes free from various conflicts and complexes. His mind becomes peaceful and he attains a higher stage of consciousness, which shows him the real path to tread and to achieve something higher he wishes to achieve. The author has used this technique of meditation for the treatment of those patients especially who are held up in the course of their development because of the repression of their spiritual urge—the so-called 'S' factor. In the case of good, honest, truthful persons who have led such a life for many years, their consciousness touches reality soon, and when it happens, problems of life pale into insignificance, intuitive ability dawns upon them and they become very useful members of society, good for themselves and good for the humanity.

References

Anthony Campbell (1980) *Seven States of Consciousness*, p.110, Victor Gollancz Ltd., London.

Dosajh, N.L. (1989), Presidential address on 'Vertical Immersion of Personality Development' delivered at the 1989th annual national conference of the India Psychological Association, held at Department of Psychology, Bharathiar University, Coimbatore – 641046.

Mahesh Yogi (1966) *The Science of Being and Art of Living*, International SRM Publication London, Frankfurt, Oslo, Geneva, Toronto, Los Angeles, Rishikesh.

Tart, Charles T. (1975) Transpersonal Psychologies, Routledge & Kegan Paul, London, p.5, 289& 434.

A Synthesis of Eastern and Western Psychology

Yoga provides a discipline whereby the disciple attains self-realisation. It is a system of mental and physical training. The methods adopted in yoga are: *Hatha Yoga, Kriya Yoga, Bhakti Yoga and Jnana Yoga or Raja Yoga,* which is a combination of all the above four. They all aim at the same goal—self-realisation. Self-realisation is the secret; self-knowledge and an increasing consciousness are the means and the process. Now, compare this with psychoanalysis in Western psychology. Whereas psychoanalysis enables one to come from the subnormal state of mind to the normal level, yoga helps not only in achieving the normal state of mind but also beyond that to the supernormal state of mind or, more accurately, to the superconscious level. This level, according to yoga philosophy, enables the 'soul' to reach its final goal of liberation. As regards the structure of the psyche, the yoga philosophy and the Western psychology have much in common. In the yoga philosophy, *Susupta* and *Swapna* states of mind may be compared to the subconscious states of mind in Western psychology, the *Jagrat* state to the conscious and the *Turia* state to the superconscious. Of course, 'superconscious state' is a new term in Western psychology, whose regions are yet to be explored in scientific terms.

As regards the contents of the psyche, there is again much in common between the two. Freud regarded the unconscious as being purely 'autogenic', i.e., the contents of the unconscious come from an individual's personal experiences, and even included racial experiences, as proposed by Jung. Jung attributed the elements in the racial unconscious to phylogenesis or race evolution. Now, according to the yoga philosophy, the *susupta* and *swapna* states of mind contain the *samskaras*, i.e., the past impressions and the impressions received from others. The one fundamental difference from the viewpoint held by Western psychologists is that according to yoga philosophy the unconscious also retains the impressions from previous lives. According to this philosophy, the human mind brings with it experiences from past lives. Even if the body dies, the *samskaras* are passed on to the new body. And it is these *samskaras* which form the basis of what we refer to as tendencies and temperaments. The Western psychology, with its emphasis on objectivity and experimental techniques, is still perfecting its tools to test the said beliefs regarding the continuance of *samskaras* of past lives and even the very viewpoint about past lives. However, Carl Jung, though a Western psychologist, comes very close to the Eastern yogis when he recognises the existence of archetypes in the human psyche. 'The theme of the archetypal images is the same in all cultures, corresponding to the phylogenetically determined portion of the human constitution... (They) stand for certain figures and contents of the collective unconscious.'

Further, 'The sum of the archetypes' signifies thus for Jung the sum of all the latent potentialities of the human psyche—an enormous, inexhaustible store of ancient knowledge concerning the most profound relations between God, man and the cosmos. To open the store to one's own psyche, to wake it to new life and to integrate it with consciousness means, therefore, nothing less than to take the individual out of his isolation and to incorporate him in the eternal cosmic process. And, so what has been sketched here becomes more than science and psychology. It becomes a teaching and a way. The archetype as precipitate of all human experiences lies in the unconscious, whence it powerfully influences our life. To release its projections, to raise its contents into consciousness, becomes a task and a duty. Now compare these ideas with parallel ideas from Yoga philosophy. Swami Vivekananda says, 'Every work that we do, every movement of the body, every thought we think, leaves such an impression on the mind, and even when such impressions are not obvious on the surface, they are sufficiently strong to work beneath the surface, subconsciously—each man's character is determined by the sum total of these impressions.' 'Within the subconscious mind lies the sum total of the experiences, impressions and tendencies of an individual, and the quality of its influence on the conscious state, as well as on the minds of others, will be determined by the quality of these impressions, according to whether or not they are good, bad or indifferent.' '— the *samskaras* of all the acts, whether of the past life or of the present, have a cumulative effect on our mind in which they are stored as latent forces but assume the form of *Vasana* or urge or active tendency when the time for their fruition comes because potential energy can become kinetic only when the proper conditions are present.' Now, as far as the presence of archetypes or samskaras in the human psyche and their influence on human personality are concerned, both the Jungian psychology and the yoga philosophy appear to be in full agreement. The main difference lies in the origin of archetypes and samskaras. Whereas Jungian archetypes are the result of inheritance of the racial unconscious, the samskaras also contain elements of the actions of past lives.

According to Jung, archetypes are self-portraits of the instincts in the psyche, as psychological processes transformed into pictures as primal patterns of human behaviour. In other words, archetypes are due to the actions of our forefather but samskaras are not only the result of the karmas of our forefathers but also the result of our own karmas during the past lives and the present one. So, the comparison between karmas and archetypes seems to break down here. But this is not a point for discouragement in the way of the unification of the Western psychology and Eastern psychology. In fact, the Yoga philosophy opens up a field for extending the horizons of the modern psychology. It opens up vast fields for research and raises questions like: Is there anything like a past life in our lives? What is soul and what does its transmigration mean? If there is or are past life or lives, whether the experiences of the past life or lives are passed on? If yes, how are these experiences passed on? Various incidents of transmigration of soul that have come to light, and a number of experiences of yogis regarding their communion with other innumerable souls are just the cases which should not be dismissed complacently or light-heartedly but given a very serious consideration, ranging from philosophic speculation to personal experiencing and, if possible, to experimenting. Psychologists have got to extend the scope of their techniques of investigation so as to include problems of the said type.

The modern techniques of experimental psychology are too inadequate to test the hypotheses of the aforesaid nature. Yogis were able to arrive at the solution of the said problems through their power of intuitive insight. And, in all phases of psychology dealing with phenomena beyond the reach of our ordinary senses, we shall have to resort to extraordinary senses like intuition etc. According to yogis, the intuitive faculty must be developed before one can answer the questions of the said type. To them, a person must be thoroughly integrated. His will is to be completely unified and made entirely active. He is expected to be firmly established in higher principles of ethics and practice of deep concentration and meditation before he can realise the truth about various incarnations. However, let us suppose that such a person makes a statement as a truth realised by him. How can we evaluate the scientific worth of his statement? The answer seems to be: by the scientific method. So ultimately, before a truth is accepted as such, it has to pass the test of the scientific method. So, even the findings of yogis as the result of their power of intuitive insight have got to fit into the framework of the scientific method before they can be accepted as scientific truths. Work is already being done and the ancient ideas on 'Thought transference, Extrasensory perception, Clairvoyance and Psychokinesis etc.' are being established by authorities like Prof. Rhine. Several of the advances in modern Western psychology are practically duplicating in their discoveries the ideas which already exist, albeit in a cruder and less scientific form, in the ancient systems. The science of psychology is already being enriched by fields like parapsychology. The ESP phenomena have definitely been proved significantly above chance. Therefore, what is needed is the formulation of proper methodology for the study of the concepts in yoga philosophy so as to bring them in line with the modern experimental psychology. It is not an easy task because the said problems do not lend themselves easily to the experimental technique. But such is the case in all new fields being explored. A method of experimentation involving intuitive apperception will have to be designed for the investigation of these extrasensory phenomena. Such a method may rightly be designated as 'Intuitive Apperception cum Experimentation'. Perhaps, the design of such experimentation could begin with the selection of the right type of persons for experiments of this nature. Persons who have developed or are gifted with the power of intuition and have a unified mind made totally active and emotionally attuned with each other will be the right sort of persons for taking up such problems. Then, the exact methodology can be worked out, depending on the problem in hand. Say, cases of parapsychology could be collected wherever possible on the surface of the earth and could be studied independently by this group of psychologists. The findings could then be compared and objectified, if possible.

Dr N.L. Dosajh

Schizophrenia: Symptoms, Aetiology and Treatment

Schizophrenia was previously known as 'dementia praecox'. This name, which meant a precocious falling away of the mind, was given by Kraepelin. However, this conception of the disease was considered to be inadequate. Bleuler as early as in 1912 pointed out that the name 'dementia praecox' was a double misnomer. Firstly, the symptoms associated with dementia praecox were observed to occur in persons of all ages - even if the highest rate of incidence tended to be between twenty and thirty years of age. Secondly, it was realised that the mental processes did not necessarily diminish progressively in their efficiency, but rather became split off from their proper relationship to social and physical reality.

Modern psychiatrists have reached the point where they can make at least fairly good transactions of the schizophrenic thought processes. It is now realised that the delusions and hallucinations, and memory defects are definitely meaningful when one considers life history. It was previously thought that dementia praecox patients rarely recover. But today we know that many do recover to the extent as they were before the overt manifestations of the sickness.

Incidence

It is reported that from 1 to 2 percent of the general population of either sex suffer from this disorder. They have relatively low recovery rate, with the result that they gradually accumulate in mental hospitals. Though it occurs in people of all age-groups, it is essentially an early age of adulthood.

Types of schizophrenia

There are four generally recognized forms of schizophrenia:

Simple Type: (Apathy) lack of emotional feeling is the main symptom. Personal hygiene is totally neglected. They rarely take bath and do not care about their dress. They talk very less. They show no interest in personal, family and communication activities.

Hebephrenic type: They suffer from emotional shallowness, childish silliness, bizarre delusions, hallucinations and confused speech. They spend hours talking and smiling to themselves or talking to imaginary persons.

Hebephrenic delusions are fantastic:

- One patient reported that a ghost had sucked out all her blood and that she was now a skeleton.
- Another patient held his breath for long periods because he felt that each time he exhaled he filled the world with poisonous gas.
- Still another person reported that there was a bee in his stomach that buzzed and talked to him.

Catatonic Type: Catatonics show either severe schizophrenic excitements or severe stupors. These may alternate or either form may predominate. The excitement is characterized by increased psychomotor activity, numerous impulsive and compulsive acts, and associations showing extreme coherence. The catatonic stupor is characterized by mutism. Apparently, the individual is psychologically completely withdrawn from reality.

Paranoid Type: This type of Schizophrenia shows the presence of other symptoms like hallucination, loss of memory, poor association of ideas, lack of interest, etc. plus paranoid delusions. It is difficult, therefore, to differentiate clearly between paranoia and the paranoid form of schizophrenia. The symptoms often overlap. The delusions are those of being persecuted – by the government, the employer, the wife etc., or of grandeur – the godman, the king, the lover, etc.

Symptoms

The symptoms of schizophrenia can be divided into primary symptoms and secondary symptoms. The symptomatology is largely based on Bleuler.

Primary Symptoms

(a) **Loosening of associations:** To a normal individual the schizophrenic's thinking often seems bizarre and unpredictable. Meehl describes this type of thinking by the apt phrase "cognitive slippage". The patient sometimes appears to employ mere fragments of ideas and concepts. He stops in the middle of a thought, or blocks in passing from one thought to another, or suddenly jumps to an irrelevant idea in the midst of a train of thought. He may combine two unrelated ideas or manifest a poverty of thinking by which he repeats a few simple ideas over and over to exclusion of others.

The schizophrenic manifests distortions of concept formation. His thinking tends to be concrete and literal.

(b) **Autistic withdrawal:** A relatively mild schizophrenic has a tenuous and unstable relation to reality. A severely disturbed schizophrenic may go further; he may completely lose touch with reality, and withdraw into a world of his own. He is preoccupied with an encapsulated world inhabited by his own wishes, fears, persecutory ideas and fantasies. Affect, thinking, speech and outside behaviour are dominated by his inner life. The aspects of external reality that filter through to him are misinterpreted and distorted. Another person's smile may be interpreted as a sneer, or a harsh comment as a sign of secret approval.

(c) **Ambivalence:** Schizophrenics are ambivalent towards themselves and others. They have a deep mistrust of people even those for whom they feel affection. A severely ill schizophrenic may strip off his clothes in front of other people while berating himself for his immodesty.

(d) Inappropriateness of Affect: Schizophrenic distortions of affect take many forms. The patient may sit with an expressive face, indicating neither pleasure nor pain and seemingly indifferent to what happens to him. On the other hand, affect is in some cases excessively labile and the patient overreacts and jumps from mood to mood. His affect may also be out of keeping with reality or with his own thoughts. If told that his wife has recovered from illness, a schizophrenic may reply, 'that is good', while the tone of his voice indicates sadness rather than joy. Conversely, disturbing news may be accepted with a smile or laughter.

Schizophrenia affect is insufficiently regulated by social standards. Some patients relate past misdeeds—real or fanciful —with no sign of shame, or use very obscene language, or masturbate openly and unconcernedly.

Secondary Symptoms

In addition to the primary symptoms, the schizophrenia may manifest some of the following secondary symptoms, which vary widely among the different diagnostic types, and among the patients within each type.

(a) **Hallucinations:** Hallucinations are false perceptions in the absence of any external source of stimulation. They are common and may involve any sense modality. If auditory, the patient hears 'voices' of imaginary persons or persons who are real but absent or silent. The voices may threaten and curse, criticise and content him. While he is eating, he may hear a voice saying, 'you ought to starve or the food will kill you'.

Visual hallucinations, sometimes called 'visions' by patients, are less common than auditory but occur in more acute phases of schizophrenia. The patient may see vague images, threatening figures, or angels and devils. Taste, smell and tactile hallucinations occur fairly often.

(b) **Delusions:** Delusions are false beliefs about one's own self. They are gross distortions of reality. The schizophrenic delusions indicate the presence of a thought disorder, but they are secondary symptoms since a thought disorder may occur without delusions.

All types of delusions occur in schizophrenia, viz., reference, influence, persecution, grandeur and so on. In patients who are depressed as well delusions of self-accusation, worthlessness and helplessness may also be found. In the delusions of grandeur, the patient may start believing that he is Lord Krishna or Jesus.

(c) **Distortions of memory:** Distortions of memory may occur in schizophrenia. The patient manifests as amnesic gap or unexpected accuracy for some long past event that had great emotional importance for him; sometimes memory is falsified rather than lost.

(d) **Speech Disorders:** A variety of speech disorders occur in schizophrenia. The patient may be mute (absence of speech) or excessively talkative or may show monotonous repetitions of words or sentences.

(e) **Motor Disturbances:** Motor disturbances occur, particularly in catatonics. The patient may be lethargic or overactive, or may manifest a musical rigidly. A patient may grimace or repeatedly perform mechanical, automatic gestures.

(f) **Anhedonia:** The schizophrenic suffers from anhedonia, an impaired capacity to experience pleasure, his interactions with others are fearful and his sexual responsiveness tends to be rudimentary and joyless. He has difficulty in feeling affection, eliciting it from others and reciprocating when it is offered.

Both the primary and secondary symptoms are regressive; i.e., indicative of a lower level of functioning than that of a mature adult. The schizophrenic's relations to other persons, his sexuality, emotionally and cognitive behaviour are infantile. He also has strong craving for protection and dependency.

Causes and Dynamics

Despite tremendous amount of research, the dynamics underlying schizophrenic disturbance is not very clear. However, some major causes are:

1. **Biological factors:** Under biological factors, factors like heredity, constitution, malfunctioning of the endocrine glands and other bodily functions are generally mentioned.

   Kallmann (1953) has pointed out that a person's chances of being a schizophrenic vary directly with the closeness of his blood relationship to a schizophrenic patient. When both the parents are schizophrenic, the expectancy rate for their children of becoming schizophrenic is 80 times that of an average person.

   Kretchmer and Sheldon have found schizophrenia to be associated with the physique of a person. They have reported schizophrenics to be slender built (asthenic type). Development irregularities are also reported in schizophrenic patients.

2. **Psychological factors:** Bleuler and others have emphasised the role of frustration and conflict in the development of schizophrenia. The individuals who develop schizophrenia, it is reported, usually manifest an early withdrawal from the world they interpret as frustrating and hostile. The mothers of male schizophrenic patients in particular are found

to be rejecting, dominating, cold, protective and unconcerned about the needs and feelings of others.

They tend to depend on their sons rather than on their fathers for their emotional satisfactions and feelings of completeness as a woman.

The mother-son relationship in schizophrenia thus appears to encourage an immature, anxious person who tends to lack a clear-cut sense of his own identity as a person with pervasive underlying feelings of inadequacy and helplessness. The fathers of schizophrenic patients are similarly found to be inadequate, indifferent, detached and humourless. They appear to be rejecting towards their son and seductive towards their daughters.

3. **Sociological factors:** Sociological difference in the incidence of schizophrenia are reported by many researchers. Schizophrenia is reported to be proportionately high among rural Africans and quite low among aborigines of Formosa. It is also observed that societies undergoing rapid social change experience a disproportionately high rate of schizophrenia.

Treatment and Prevention

Modern drugs – tranquilizers and energizers – have proved quite effective in the treatment of schizophrenia.

These drugs are used in combination with electric shock therapy to greater advantage.

Operant conditioning methods are also used in the treatment of schizophrenic patients with promising results.

The aetiology and pathogenesis of schizophrenia in various cultures are shrouded in mystery. Various attempts have been made to unravel this mystery. Genetic factors have been studied but still no specific genes have been embarked which could be said to cause schizophrenia. Many twin studies and studies of adopted children have merely led to very conflicting results making the issue more complicated. The psychological studies have simply added to the number of symptoms and their classifications without throwing much light on the aetiology of the disorder. The biochemical studies have been able to identify certain chemicals in the urine and sweat of the schizophrenics but the issue whether these chemicals are the result of the disorder remains unexplained. The complete cure of schizophrenia is still not known because of its manifold complexities. Of course, there are many psychopharmacological agents that have been tried but out of the many possible outcomes, a majority of schizophrenics emerge in the categories of social remission with frequent relapses. Even western Psychotherapies have not ensured complete cure. A combination of Psychotherapy and Drug Therapy has proved more effective than either of two. Even programs of after-care combined with adequate dose of Fluphenazine Enanthate (Prolixin Enanthate) have been found to be the treatment of choice, yet even this combination was not able to prevent the relapse of this disorder. In an effort to have better management, the researcher tried the use of yoga therapy in combination with other therapies and evolved this new technique based on Eastern and Western psychotherapies presented here, which has been tried on more than ten cases leading to better management.

1.   **Drug Therapy:** To manage violent patient by psychiatrist.

2.   **Psychotherapy:** Here we use techniques like psychoanalysis, cognitive therapy, suggestion, etc. The nature of the technique employed will depend upon the nature of the patient.

3.   **Yoga Therapy:** As soon as we find that the patient has sufficiently improved and accepts different therapies, he may be put on yoga therapy. Yoga helps in total eradication of mental conflicts, unpleasant urges and tendencies.

4.   **Evaluation:** Evaluation of the patient's progress is done from time to time by administering the Rorschach test. For illustration, one case is enumerated below:

Case of Schizophrenia treated by Eastern and Western Techniques

It is the case of a woman aged 32 years. She was a graduate, married and had a son. Her husband was an Air Force officer, and father a retired Army officer. She had been diagnosed as a case of schizophrenia. At the time of her contact with me, she was full of fears and had hatred for her father to the extent that at times she felt like killing him. She lacked confidence in talking to others. She would not mix with her neighbours. Her mother-in-law suffered from depression. During her childhood and adolescence, she was nagged by her father and kept shut indoors. She was not allowed to mix freely with people outside her house. She had to pass through a very submissive childhood. She was educated up to B.A., but in school and college a strict supervision was kept on her. Father, instead of giving love, rebuked her, especially when he was drunk. Mother was of an irritable temperament and father and mother often used to quarrel over trifles. Her husband was posted away from home and so met her only on holidays, otherwise she stayed with her in-laws. She hated sex life and this often irritated the husband. After the birth of one child, she had problem of infertility. She liked to live alone and did not like to accompany her husband where he was posted. In early life she had a passionate attraction towards one of her classmates. She used to sleep with her and the two would kiss each other, it developed into a lesbian relationship. They would fondle each other's breasts and then she would have erotic feelings. Then at times she would masturbate. She did not like to meet that class-fellow now. During her college life she became fond of novels depicting incidents of murder and ghosts' stories. She often dreamt about her remarriage and her other dreams showed lot of anxiety about her only child. She would also often dream that she has another baby born to her. Also, another dream that she often had was having sexual intercourse with elder brother of her husband.

She was administered Rorschach Test in September 1984. The first administration showed the following characteristics:

1) 10 W responses but vague; 2) Human content-1; 3) No human movement; 4) Anatomical responses-4; 5) There was complete vagueness of percept; 6) There was lot of perseverance; 7) Her protocol showed 4 bones; 8) There were 4 pure colour responses; 9) There was one blood response; 10) Total number of responses were twelve.

Treatment

She was first under the treatment of a psychiatrist who administered her Eskazine and Calmpose. The patient was not happy with the psychiatrist, hence changed the therapist and came to the author who administered psychotherapy to her. After about one month of psychotherapy, she was administered the Rorschach test and results are shown below:

1) 10 W responses but vague; 2) Human content-(H)3; 3) Human movement-1; 4) Anatomical responses -5; 5) Vagueness of percept present; 6) Perseverance was there but less than last administration; 7) Bones -4; 8) Colour responses – 7; 9) Blood responses-2; 10) Total number of responses – 39.

She was trained in yoga therapy. She learned shavasan, padamasan, pranayama, cobra pose, etc. After about 4 months she was again administered Rorschach test and the results were as under:

1) 7 W response with good form level; 2) Human Content – (H)-1; 3) Human Movement -; 4) Anatomical response-1; 5) Percept on the whole – good; 6) Perseveration – once only; 7) Bones -1; 8)

Colour responses – 4; 9) Blood responses -1; 10) Total responses – 31.

She was asked to continue yogic exercises. In May 1985, she informed me that she was alright, thus she would like to terminate therapy as she wanted to join her husband.

Follow-up (One Year): She was staying with her husband happily.

In short, with new treatment methods, it is reported that half of all first admissions get discharged within 4 months, two-thirds within 6 months and 90 percent within year.

References

Dosajh N. L. (1978): *'D' Test, and Rorschach Test as Evaluation Tools in the treatment of A Schizophrenic Patient*, Journal of Rajasthan Psychiatric Society, 5, 28-35.

Dosajh N.L. (1983). *Psychotherapy including 'Yoga Therapy'*, Kohli Publishers, 3 Industrial Area, Phase-II, Chandigarh-160002

Dosajh N.L. (1986): *Treatment of A cast of Schizophrenia (undifferentiated with the Help of Western Psychotherapies and Yoga*, Paper read at the XVI conference of Indian Association of Psychologists held at Dr Hari Singh Gour, Vishwavidyalaya, Sagar (MP).

Dosajh N.L. (1988): *Synthesis of Eastern & Western Psychotherapies* unpublished SP Eastern-Western Psychology National Award Lecture.

Michael Goldstein, Eliot H Rodnick, Jerome, R Erans, Philips R.A. May and Mark Steinberg (1978). *Drug and family Therapy in the Aftercare.* Treatment of Acute Schizophrenia, University of California Los Angeles.

Perry W.G. (1976): On the relation of Psychotherapy to counselling.

In G.S Balkin (Ed). *Counselling, Directions in Theory and Practice*, Dubugue Iowar: Kenda/Hunt.

Sinha A.K.P (1985): *Eastern and Western Psychotherapies*, Ind. J. Psychology, 60, 1-22

(Courtesy: Psy & Mental Health) 1995, 2, 135-138.

'D' (Dosajh) Test

This test was originally designed as a parallel form of the H.H (Hellersberg) test (1945). The 'D' test has been standardised stage-wise

First Stage: The test was administered to more than 1000 normal subjects.

Second Stage: The test was administered to psychoneurotics.

Third Stage: The test was administered to psychotics.

A number of papers were published in various journals e.g. (i) Indian journal of psychology; (ii) Research bulletin of International Institute of Child Study Bangkok 1957; (iii) Indian Journal of Clinical Psychology and (iv) Journal of Rajasthan Psychiatric Society.

Description of the test

The test consists of four sheets of paper. There are three sheets having four rectangles on each and then there is a fourth sheet with a blank rectangle. All rectangles on the first pages have different sorts of lines which are quite haphazard and seem absolutely meaningless. Rectangle 'A' has small curved line in the top left corner and two other lines, three are rather curvilinear but the fourth is completely haphazard. There are two angular lines in rectangle 'C'. Similarly, rectangle 'D' has two curved and one wavy line and so on.

Procedure

The following instructions in a printed form were given to the subject:

1. You are provided with three sheets of paper and in them there are 12 rectangles. Each rectangle has some signs. With the help of these signs, make a picture in each rectangle with pencil by adding something of your own. After finishing each picture write under it, its name and the order in which you have made it i.e. write down, 1 under the first picture that you make, 2 under the second, 3 under the third and so on. Do not worry about your ability in drawing but draw something that comes to your mind. Also mention under each what is going on in the picture that you have drawn. You may turn the rectangles in any direction you like.

2. The maximum time allowed is 1 ½ hours but you try to finish it as quickly as you can, sooner the better.

3. If you have to ask anything, gently tap your table but do not leave your seat (as soon as there was tapping, the examiner went near the subject).

4. After you have finished the three sheets, ask for the fourth sheet.

While the subject takes the test, the examiner fills out the 'Observation Form'. The idea of filling the 'Observation Form' is to get information about the behaviour of the subject during the test.

It is presumed that every aspect of behaviour has some significance. Gestures, emotional responses, tensions on the face, leaving the task incomplete, losing temper, changing mood, impulsiveness etc. all have great significance and are important points to be taken note of. While the subject is drawing, he is also presenting a particular type of behaviour. He makes certain remarks, changes the expression of his face, feels restless or calm etc. all these are important. It is not only the drawing in which we are interested but also the way the subject behaves.

One of the things we look for is the amount of projection the subject shows in his drawings and the idea of providing the fourth sheet having a blank rectangle is to afford the subject with a greater opportunity to project himself, if at all he wants to project.

A

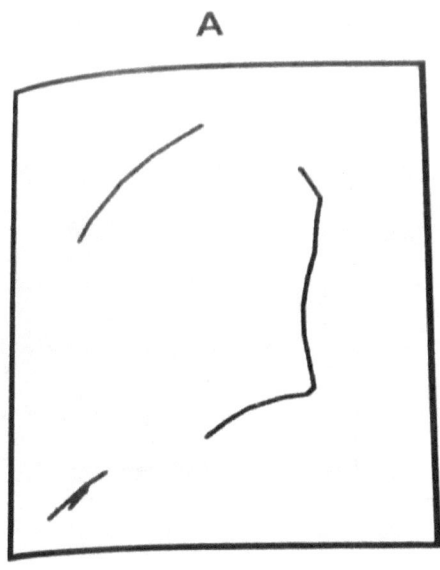

B

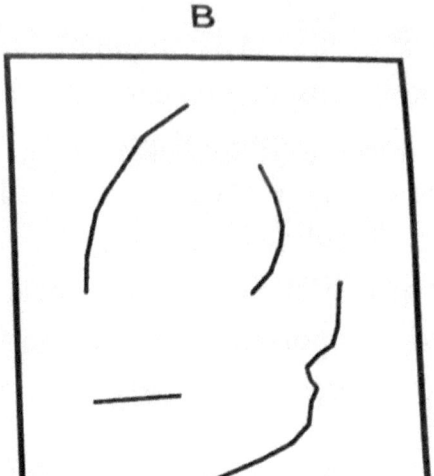

C

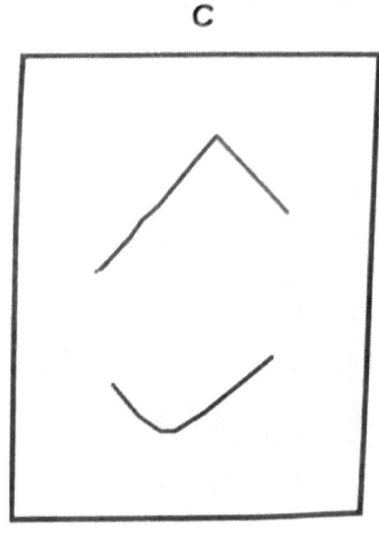

D

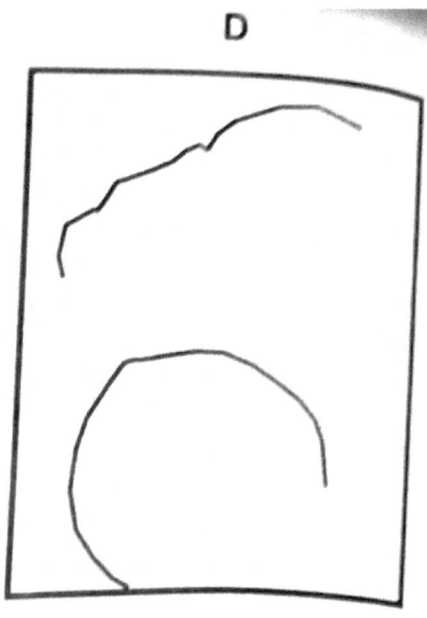

E

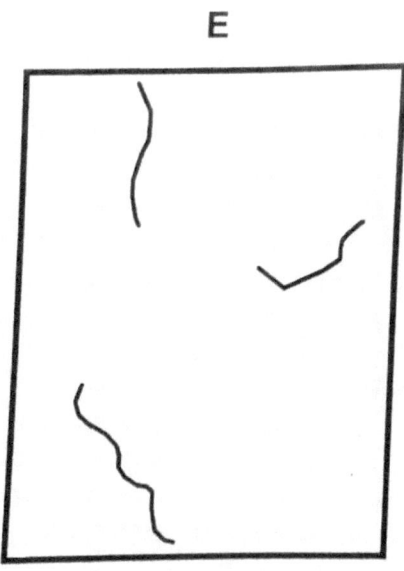

F

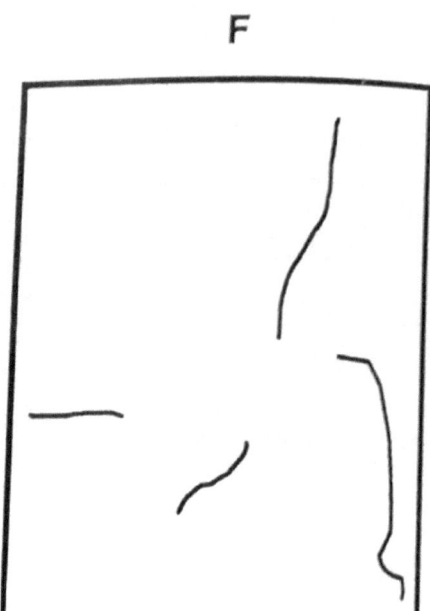

G

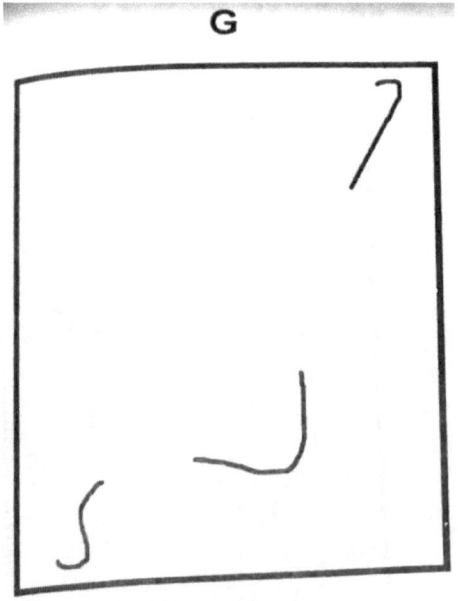

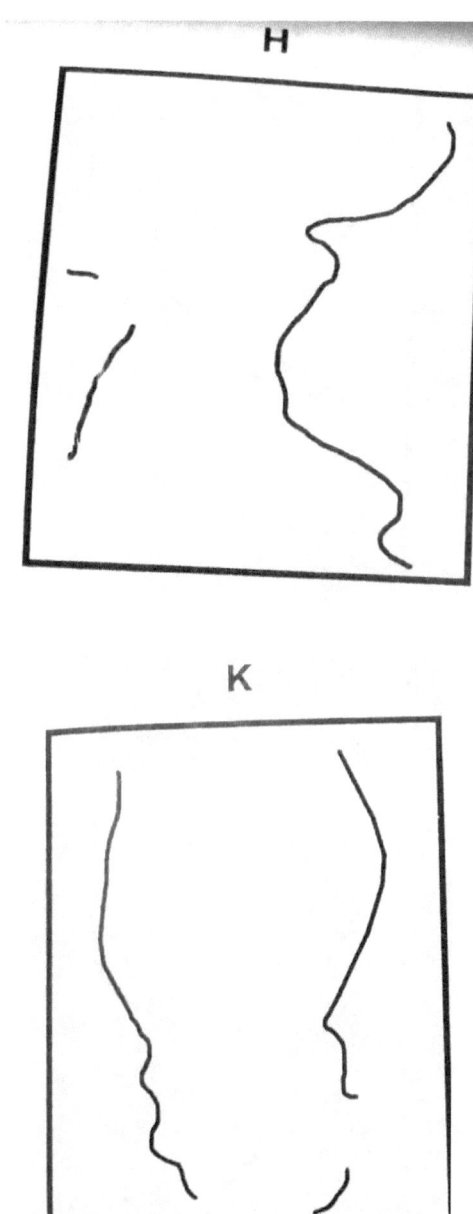

L

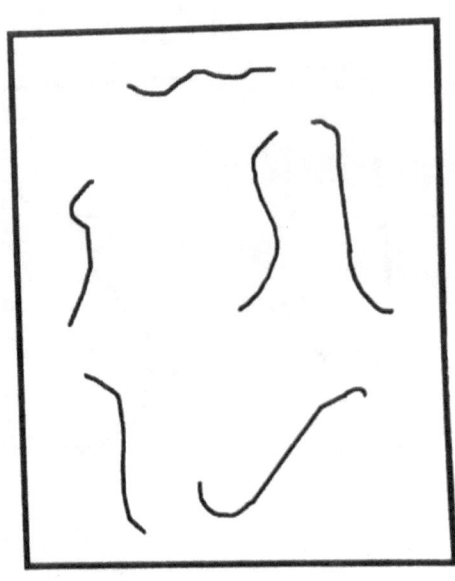

M

N

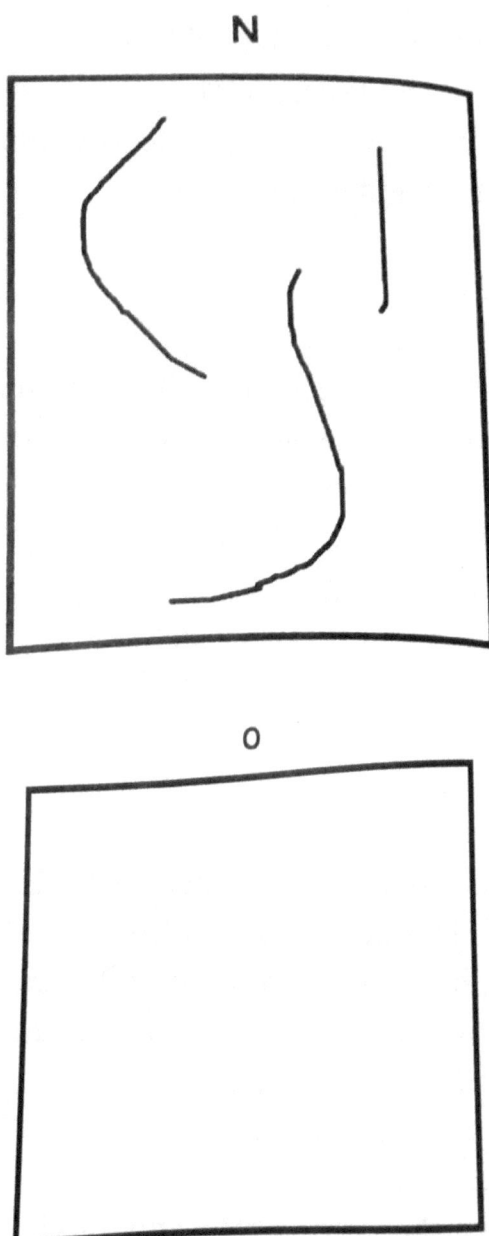

O

Observation Form

General Behaviour of the Subject

A. Is the subject taking rest?

1. Readily: when the subject feels willingness, without reluctance and hesitation.

    Yes............................

    Undecided............................

    No.............

2. With a set in the mind: When the subject feels that he anticipates what he is doing to perceive and completes the test in no time.

    Yes................. Undecided............................

    No.................

3. Without Interest: When the subject is not in a state of engaged attention and curiosity.

    Yes...................... Undecided

    ....

    No......................

B. Are his movements spontaneous?............................

    When the subject's movements are involuntary, acting by its own impulse or natural law, a sort of reflex which is not under his voluntary control.

    Yes............................ Undecided

    ....

    No......................

4. Does he show stereotype activities?

5. Does the subject show the same form of expression and movements towards all the drawings or has

different expressions and movements while making different drawings?

Yes...................   Undecided

....

No.............................

Often.............................

Occasional ....

6. Does the subject leave the task deliberately due to

(i) Blockage............... Yes.........................

No...............

(ii) Boredom............................

Yes.............................

No...................

Motivation

1. How many times does the subject require encouragement for drawing?

A...........................

E.............................

K.............................

B.........................

F............................

J............................. O...................

C......................... G............................

M.............................

D........................... H...................

N...............................

2. No. of times the subject shows distraction in each figure

A...........................

E..............................

K..............................

B...........................

F...............................

J............................ O.....................

C......................... G............................

M...........................

D......................... H............................

N................................

3. Does he complete the task without encouragement?

Yes...................... Undecided

....

No............................

4. Does he leave the task in between?

Yes.........................

Undecided.............................

No......................

5. Does he feel the presence of the tester?

Yes............................. Undecided

No...............................

ANY OTHER REMARKS

....

....

....

....

....

....

....
....
....

The following procedure was adopted for the administration of the test:

1. Preferably the test was given individually.

2. The subject was made to sit comfortably.

3. The examiner went to the seat of the subject, handed over the three sheets and the Instructions Sheet to the subject.

4. After handing over the test sheet and the 'instructions to the subject' sheet, the examiner sat a little away from the subject towards his back. In no case did the examiner sit facing the subject.

5. After 15 minutes he checked whether the subject was proceeding all right.

6. Immediately after the subject had finished the test, the examiner went through what the subject had written under each drawing so as to see what the subject had drawn.

7. The question that the candidate asked and the answers given by the examiner, subject's gestures, facial expression, motor movements and his other behaviours during the test were recorded by the examiner in the observation form.

8. Some of the questions that the subjects asked and the answers that were given are as follows: -

    i. The golden rule which was kept in mind while answering the question was not to suggest anything but to let the subject use its own discretion. Answers like just as you please', 'you may do as you like', 'yes', 'do as you think proper', etc, were frequently given.

ii.   If the subject enquired if his picture was right, he was told that from it a number of pictures could be drawn each one according to one's individuality.

iii. If he said that he could not make the picture and that he had never done this before, then he was told 'we do not expect drawing ability from you, we simply want to see what you make.'

iv. If it was observed that the subject was proceeding very slowly, then he was told that there was no need for him to go slow. He should try to draw quickly.

v.   If he said that his picture was not clear, he was told that it did not matter.

vi.   If he enquired whether he could go beyond the boundary line, he was told it depended upon him, he could do whatever he liked.

vii. If he asked whether he should make an animal, a man or a plant, then he was told that it was entirely his own outlook. If he experienced a great difficulty in drawing and was stuck up and said that he could not draw then he was encouraged but he was not helped in the least in making a drawing. If he said whether he should make one figure or many figures in each rectangle then he was told, "Preferably one'.

(The subject was provided with black pencil, different sorts of colour pencils and eraser).

After the test is complete, an interview is held. Each rectangle is taken in the order in which subject completed them. The interview is so directed as to find out first what it was that gave the idea, secondly, to see the thinking process and thirdly, to see if there was any symbolic material in the drawings.

On the basis of his drawings and the interview the person was categorised into five levels keeping in mind two of the traits. Imagination and maturity.

Imagination

I. **Category:** Definitely active, creative imagination shows originality in at least four rectangles – depicts abstract idea, sketches scenes, illustrates a principle or law or produces some new design characterised by a high quality of form accuracy, organisation and combination of elements with enlivening of sketches by form illustrations and at least three different responses. The ratio between the popular (P)* and (O)** response P/O is generally 0.30 or less.

* By popular (P) responses is meant those responses that occur at least 6 times in the same rectangle in a record of about 600 subjects.

** By 'Original' (O) responses is meant those responses which do not resemble the popular responses and are well fitted to the given lines.

II. **Category:** Accurate form, organisation and combination of elements in at least four rectangles but no form elaboration, at least 2 different varieties in the nature of responses. The value of P/O generally ranges from 0.31 to 0.75.

III. **Category:** Vague form, poor organisation and not complete combination of elements in 8 or more than 8 rectangles. The value of P/O generally ranges from 0.76 to 1.30.

IV. **Category:** Form loose, no organisation, combination of elements poor in 10 or more of the rectangles. The value of P/O generally ranges from 1.31 to 3, sometimes more than 3.

V. **Category:** Predominance of simple, discrete, childish uncoordinated sketches. The subject fails to make one complete picture in one rectangle (excluding rectangle 'O') but makes 2 or more pictures having no relation with either spatial or verbal or totally fails to make use of the given lines. (At least 12 rectangles are counted for scoring).

Maturity

A human concept or a human attribute shown in the rectangle symbolises the interest in the people around and, consequently, shows a rapport with the world outside or refers to the ability of an individual to chat or identify with others. The projection of human responses, within the context of a good tie to reality, shows a high level of emotional maturity.

People identify themselves less readily with animals than with human figures but the kind of affects or attitudes expressed in regard to animals may represent the fantasy life of the individuals. The drawings of animals indicate a lack of capacity for creativity. It simply means common and stereotype. Mere representation of animal responses in the case of an adult merely indicates a paucity of interest. On the basis of human and animal responses, the following levels of emotional maturity have been demarcated.

Category I: The value of $2M + A/N^*$ is above 1.0

Category II: The value of $2M + A/N$ ranges from 0.51 to 1.0

Category III: The value of $2M + A/N$ ranges from 0.31 to 0.5

Category IV: In the responses either there might be some true projection** or the value of $2M + A/N$ may range from 0.10 to 0.30 or both or there are no 'M' or 'A' responses.

Category V: Manner of approach may be impulsive, restless, may be mostly distracted and may often leave his task unfinished, may need encouragement often. Facial expression may show excitement; may take unnecessary gestures and movements. The value of $2M + A/N$ is below 0.10.

*M stands for human figures or figures in humanlike action. Mythological figures or animals when they are depicted behaving as human beings. A stands for animal figures. N stands for the total number of rectangles completed by the subject.

** In true projection it is assumed that there is always some element of the unpleasant, the unwanted and the morally undesirable about the projected trait.

Some Popular Concepts of the 'D' Test

Rectangle A: Birds, coasts, maps (geographical), mountain, river, leaf, hill, rat, snake, crow, sparrow, clouds, face, tree, curve, duck, pigeon, gas balloon, woman, face of a man.

Rectangle B: Flower, rivers, trees, mountains, face, man, sitting on a chair, snake, cartoon, map of India, map, man, human hips, girl human being, roads.

Rectangle C: Arrow, axe, birds 57, flowers, flasks, inkpot, trees, triangle, bow, racket, sickle, mountain, rat, rock, flower, plant, flag, landscape, boy, kite, scenery.

Rectangle D: Maps (Geographical), clouds, flowers, leaf, Suez Canal, flag, river, jug, tree, island, human, animal, girl, human being.

Rectangle E: Aeroplane, clouds, mountains, rivers, rain falling, map of Burma, India, Punjab, South America, man sitting, clouds, hill, map, human face, girl, flower.

Rectangle F: Clouds, clouds in the sky, flower, leaf, man, mountain, snake or serpent, camel, river, map of India, tree, axe, hook, boat, missile.

Rectangle G: Quadrupeds, bow and arrow, trees. house, map of India, mountain, animal, crossing and the road, South India, dog, spaceship.

Rectangle H: Clouds, flowers, island, leaves, man, map of Burma, tree, bat, map of India, rock, scenery, girl, child, woman.

Rectangle K: Mountains, map of the Deccan, India, East and West Coasts of India, America, South America and South Africa, map, baby, girl, hill, man, boy, tributaries.

Rectangle L: Trees, dried tree, old tree, flowers, head, man, trees, rivers, zigzag, animal, face, girl, bloom, floral diagram, lady.

Rectangle N: House, leg, waterfall, letter box, national flag, mountains, man, cat, index finger, pigeon.

Rectangle O: Flower pot, flower, rose, leaf, poem, tree, woman, book, map of India, mango, man, national flag, glass of water, scenery, aeroplane, boy.

Scoring

The score of the subject was counted in levels, e.g. a person who is placed in category I is considered to have scored 1 point. The higher the score, the worse it is and lower the score the better it is for the individual. Point 1 score is considered to be the best of all scores.

Reliability

The reliability was determined with the help of the parallel form. The co-efficient or co-relation for reliability comes to .64 for imagination and 0.62 for maturity.

Validity

For determining the validity, the standard Rorschach Test was used. For scoring of RR the following procedure was adopted: -

For imagination, the procedure adopted is nearly the same as adopted by Klopfer and Kelley for estimating of intellectual level, since imagination has been taken to mean intellectual level. The estimate of imagination is based mainly on the number and quality of W, number and quality of M, form accuracy level, number and quality of original responses of the subject.

Levels of imagination have been based on the Rorschach's findings that a relatively high number of W's, represents the higher forms of mental activity. Of course, taking into consideration the form level and organisation.

Category I: At least 3 Ws* of superior construction, 5 or more M (responses, generally more than 50% W's).

Category II: Ws at least 3, most of them organised. About 3 M responses 30-50% W's.

Category III: Mostly 'crude' determinant Ws, 20-30% Ws.

Category IV: Mostly unrelated, inaccurate outline 10-20% Ws.

Category V: Inaccurate, unorganised outline Ws, may have confabulatory Ws as well Ws generally less than 10%.

The validity coefficient for imagination and emotional maturity come to 0.78 and 0.69 respectively.

Levels of maturity have been framed on the basis of "Emotional Aspects of Personality" as revealed by Klopfer and Kelley in chapter 12 of the book, *Rorschach Technique* (1942).

Meaning of symbols

*The meaning of the various symbols used is the same as given by Klopfer and Kelley. The Rorschach Technique (1942)

Briefly the meanings are: -

W – Whole blot area

M – Human or humanlike movement

F – Form

W – When the subject discovers a clear form of a part of the object in a tiny portion of the blot and declares the whole of the blot as that object although there is no resemblance.

Category I: Preponderance of FC** responses over CF**. M responses of good quality involving the perception of real human figures and in optimal relationship to FM**

Category II: Even distribution of all degree responses, FC greater than CF, M nearly 3.

Category III: FC responses are equal to CF responses.

Category IV: m is greater than M plus FM and generally more than 3, there may be diffusion of responses (K)*, toned down shading effects (k)* may show crude 'C" responses or colour naming (Cn). There may be pathological responses as well.

For a more detailed account of the D-test read 'D' (DOSAJH) TEST by Dr N.L. Dosajh, published by Mahavir International, 1025, Sector 15 B, Chandigarh

Appendix

Untiring Healer Of The Mind

When it is normal for most living beings to suffer from some kind of physical ailment, human beings are unique for they suffer from a number of disorders that do not appear to have a physical cause, these are mental disorders. And there are doctors who specialise in treating such disorders. Dr N.L. Dosajh has spent his entire life in the service of those who are tormented by the demons of the mind.

'Mental health is a very serious matter', cautions Dr Dosajh, 'unfortunately, in our country we do not take it seriously. There is a stigma attached to seeing a psychiatrist. If mental health is neglected, it could lead to serious problems. After a stage, the patient could become a problem not only to the society but also to himself. Professional help should be sought at the earliest.'

Although nudging ninety, Dosajh refuses to call it a day. The main cause of mental ill health, the doctor says, is a drop in the level of consciousness. 'When consciousness is at higher levels, an individual is in perfect mental health, but when it drops to lower levels, neurosis is the result, and the lower you go the more neurotic you become. The major reasons for the weakening of consciousness are repression, conflicts, complexes, frustrations and setbacks in life.'

To get to the root of the mental disorder, Dosajh interviews the patient as well as the family and friends. Often, the repression is so severe that there is a great resistance from the patient to reveal the inner conflicts as most of them are sex-related. Usually, the patient is totally unaware of them, and is unable to tell the doctor anything much about the problem. In such cases, various methods are used to delve into the unconscious of the patient. 'I use free association, Rorschach inkblot test, hypnosis and so on. If none of them work, I try to get clues from the patient's dreams. Or, I might ask the patient to make up a story, and from the patient's imaginations I get hints about the cause of neurosis. It is only after a thorough analysis I decide on the right technique to be used for a cure, which varies from patient to patient, upon the seriousness of the disorder and so on. There are no short-cuts or readymade formulas here.'

Using his wide experience, Dr Dosajh devised his own test called the D-Test. 'When you undergo a D-Test,' explains the doctor, 'three sheets of paper with 12 rectangles are presented to you. Each rectangle has a few lines on it. You are asked to make further additions to the lines and draw any figure that occurs to you. You have about an hour and a half to finish the drawing. It is not necessary to complete this test.' Based on the figures drawn by the patient, Dr Dosajh gets clues to the unconscious cause of their neurosis, and only then he decides on the nature of cure, be it stress-relieving exercises like yoga and meditation, autosuggestion, hypnosis or, in some cases, medication. 'But I try to avoid the use of medicines as much as possible. I prefer rejuvenating the life force and the mental energy of the patient.' With these improvised techniques, the doctor has cured dozens of patients suffering from schizophrenia, personality disorders and so on.

The major influence on Dr Dosajh's life is Carl Jung, on whose theories he has based his own work. Others who inspired him are Sigmund Freud, G. Murphy and the behaviourist, B.F. Skinner. Dosajh realised that the Indian tradition offered many effective techniques, and it was worthwhile including them in his therapy. Interaction with Shri Akhand Swami of Gangotri in the late 1930s, and Swami Sivanand in the 1950s, further honed his skills. He was also greatly influenced by the teachings of Swami Akhilanand, Geraldine Coster, Shri Aurobindo, Mahesh Yogi, Bloomfield Harold and Kory Robert B. Using the foundations of western psychology and Indian systems, he fused yoga and meditation with psychoanalysis to create his own theory which he calls the New Personality Theory.

In his long career, Dr Dosajh was recognised by the professional community in many ways. In 1956, he was sent as a UNESCO Fellow to work at the International Institute of Child Study at Bangkok and was a Guest Professor at the PGI for over 20 years.

(*Excerpts from an article by Dr Kuldip Dhiman that appeared in The Tribune, June20, 2004*)

About the author

(Dr N.L. Dosajh 1916-2005)

In his long career, Dr Dosajh was recognised by the professional community in many ways. In 1956, he was sent as a UNESCO Fellow to work at the International Institute of Child Study at Bangkok and was a Guest Professor at the PGI for over 20 years. Using the foundations of western psychology and Indian systems, he fused yoga and meditation with psychoanalysis to create his own theory which he calls the New Personality Theory. With improvised techniques, the doctor cured dozens of patients suffering from schizophrenia, personality disorders and so on.

This book can be of immense value to students and researchers in the field of Psychology, as well as to the professional psychiatrists and psychotherapists.